DK

AN ANTHOLOGY OF

Fungi

WARNING: This book is an introduction to the amazing world of fungi, and is for general information purposes only. It is not a guide to foraging mushrooms, which the publisher would expressly discourage unless each mushroom to be picked has been identified by an expert. This book has not specifically identified poisonous or edible fungi, and the advice for any fungi spotting is ***Look but don't touch!***, as fungi can cause allergic reactions to skin or be poisonous to touch. Under no circumstances can the authors and the publisher accept any liability for any death, injury, or damage arising out of touching or eating any fungi.

AN ANTHOLOGY OF

Fungi

Written by Ali Ashby and Lynne Boddy
Illustrated by Angela Rizza and Daniel Long

Contents

Bristly tropical cups (Cookeina tricholoma) are ascomycetes.

Horsehair mushrooms (Gymnopus androsaceus) are basidiomycetes.

Welcome to the Fungi kingdom

Fungi are not plants, bacteria, or viruses. They are not animals, either—although they are more closely related to them than they are to plants. Fungi have their very own kingdom and there are probably at least five million of them, though only about 150,000 species have been named so far. These have been divided into many groups, based on their DNA and different visual features.

Phycomyces blakesleeanus belongs to the group Mucoromycota. It breaks down animal dung.

Naming fungi

Plants, animals, and fungi all have scientific names—which come mostly from Latin and Greek, and tend to be written in sloping, italic letters. These names have two parts, such as *Boletus edulis*, and often tell us something about the shape, color, or another feature of the fruit body. Many fungi also have common names, in local languages.

Fungi groups

Most of the fungi in this book belong to two main groups—called basidiomycetes and ascomycetes. The fruit body of a fungus is the part where spores are made, and the fruit bodies of these two groups are usually big enough to see at some point in their life cycles. Other fungal groups have members that are so small they can only be seen with a microscope.

The English common name of *Boletus edulis* is "penny bun," because its shiny brown cap looks like a penny bun—a small bread loaf that used to be sold for a penny.

Microscopic *Batrachochytrium dendrobatidis*, which is wiping out amphibians, is part of a group called Chytridiomycota.

7

Fruit body shapes

Fungal fruit bodies can be different sizes, shapes, textures, and colors. Some can only be seen with a microscope, yet others are more than 3 ft (1 m) wide! They can be sorted by shape and whether spores are made inside them or outside—in tubes or on gills, spines, or other surfaces.

Mushrooms

"Mushroom" refers to a fruit body's shape—it does not mean the fruit body is safe to eat. Mushrooms have a stem supporting a cap, with gills, tubes, or spines on the underside. Spores are made on the gills or spines, or inside the tubes, which show as pores.

Cap

Gills

Stem

Verdigris waxcap (Gliophorus viridis)

Shelves and brackets

The fruit bodies of these wood-decay fungi grow out of tree trunks, branches, fallen twigs, or stumps. They look like shelves. Some grow very large—the giant elm bracket can be 3 ft (1 m) across.

Spores are made inside upright tubes, here. The hole at the end of the tube is the pore.

Giant elm bracket (Rigidoporus ulmarius)

Crusts

These flat, basidiomycete fruit bodies form on the underside of wood. They can be smooth or have spines or warts.

Blue is a rare color in the fungal kingdom.

Cobalt crust (*Terana coerulea*)

Stinkhorns

These fruit bodies emerge from a white egg, which is often buried in the soil. The spores are made in smelly slime on the fruit body, which attracts flies. The slime sticks to the flies, and the spores spread to new places.

Anemone stinkhorn (*Aseroe rubra*)

Corals and clubs

Corals and clubs produce spores on the surface of their fruit bodies. The violet coral fungus makes its spores on the surface of coral-like branches that are rounded at the tips.

Violet coral fungus (*Clavaria zollingeri*)

Cups, saddles, ears, and fingers

These are some of the fruit bodies made by ascomycete fungi. The spores are made in tiny sacs on the upper surface of soft cups, or saucer- or saddle-shaped fruit bodies. Or they are made in sacs in the outer layer of hard fingers or balls. Often the spores are shot out of the fruit body with force, so these types of fungi are sometimes called the spore shooters.

Spores are made in sacs on the inner surface.

Hare's ear fungus (*Otidea onotica*)

Spores are made inside tiny, flask-shaped structures on the surface of each finger.

Dead man's fingers (*Xylaria polymorpha*)

Fans

These basidiomycete fungi make beautiful, fan-shaped fruit bodies. The spores are produced on the paler underside of the fan.

Fan-shaped fruit bodies

Earth fan (*Thelephora terrestris*)

Jelly and rubbery fungi

These basidiomycete fungi have rubbery fruit bodies. The fruit bodies often dry out, but then become rubbery again after rainfall. They can be smooth or have spines or warts.

The spores are formed on the paler surface underneath the funnel.

Salmon salad fungus (*Guepinia helvelloides*)

Puffballs, earthstars, and earthballs

Spores are made inside these ball- or onion-shaped fruit bodies. The spores puff out from a hole at the top of puffballs and earthstars, when a twig or drop of rain lands on them. With earthballs, the outside layer splits to let the spores spread.

Spores puff out of a hole that forms at the top.

A brown puffball stump is left when the spores have been shed.

Mosaic puffball (*Bovistella utriformis*)

The outer layer of an earthstar cracks into different parts, which bend backward into stilts that lift the inner ball up.

Barometer earthstar (*Astraeus hygrometricus*)

Decayers

Fungal filaments, called hyphae, release enzymes that break down dead plant parts and other material into smaller food molecules that they can then absorb. Decayers are our planet's best recyclers because they release nutrients into the soil that plants and other microbes can use for growth.

How fungi live

Most plants can make their own food—but fungi cannot. Instead, many fungi find food such as wood or leaves. These foods are too big to be absorbed whole, so fungi first send out special chemicals, called enzymes, which break them down into smaller parts. Other fungi get ready-made food, which doesn't need to be broken down, in the form of sugars from a plant partner.

Partners with plant roots

Most plants have fungi in their roots. The fungi grow out into the soil and get water and nutrients from areas the plant roots cannot reach. The water and nutrients are swapped for sugars from the plants. These fungi can often rot dead leaves to get extra food.

Partners with animals

Some ants, termites, wood wasps, and beetles team up with fungi. The animals bring food to the fungi or take them to it. In return, the fungi soften the food or break it down so the animals can digest it.

The fruit bodies of some *Cordyceps* fungi grow from insects they have killed.

Parasites and killers

Some fungi, called parasites, get their food by growing on living plants. Others feed on parts of plants, whole plants, or insects that they have killed.

This diagram shows how fungal hyphae wrap around green algal cells inside the lichen.

Lichen

Lichens are fungi that team up with green algae and cyanobacteria, which feed them carbohydrates. The fungi, in return, protect the partners and provide them with water and nutrients. Lichens look a little like plants or crusts on rocks.

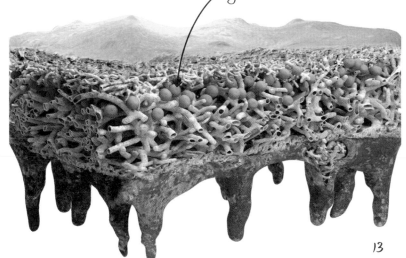

Grasslands and meadows

Grassy areas, such as fields, road shoulders, and lawns, have their own sets of fungi. Some fungi can live in many types of grasslands, but others are only found in one type of soil. For example, a fungus might need to live in soil that is home to certain types of plants, or it might prefer grassland grazed by animals. Mushrooms aren't the only clue that a fungus is living in the soil beneath grass—a ring of lush grass, or of dead grass or bare soil, can also be evidence that a fungus is present. Read on to discover some of the fungi found in these habitats.

Field mushroom
Agaricus campestris

When they first appear out of the ground, field mushrooms look like the button mushrooms you might see in supermarkets—which are close relatives. Their caps get larger as they grow, and open out to reveal plate-like gills. They usually appear scattered across fields and on grassy shoulders, though sometimes they grow in fairy rings. They feed on dead plant material and grass roots in the soil.

The gills are pink when young, but turn dark brown.

Yellow stainer

Agaricus xanthodermus

It is easy to spot the yellow stainer because the mushroom turns a bright-yellow color if the stem or cap is bruised or cut. It is a poisonous relative of the common field mushroom. The yellow stainer's scientific name is *Agaricus xanthodermus*, which comes from the Greek words for yellow (*Xanthos*) and skin (*dermis*).

The flesh bruises yellow.

The caps are 2–6 in (5–15 cm) across.

The caps are ball-shaped to begin with, but flatten with age.

The gills are pink when young, but turn gray-brown with age.

St. George's mushroom

Calocybe gambosa

This pretty, stocky mushroom appears on or around the English Patron Saint Day of St. George's Day (April 23), which is why it was given its common name. Part of the mushroom's scientific name is the Latin word *Calocybe*, which means "pretty head." It looks similar to the deadly poisonous fibercap fungus— but the fibercap has different colored gills and fibers on its cap.

Notes

· Cap 2-6 in (5-15 cm) across

· White spore print (see glossary)

· Appears spring through to early summer

The smooth caps are cream and often irregularly shaped.

The stem is slightly thicker at the base.

Giant puffball

Calvatia gigantea

The fruit bodies of these gigantic fungi often look like oversized, wrinkled soccerballs. They are very easy to spot on grassy shoulders, woodland edges, and grassland—often in small groups, and sometimes forming fairy rings. In ancient times, strips of the fungus were used to stop bleeding, like a fungal bandage. The fungus was also used to light fires or to carry flames, and beekeepers lit it to create smoke that calmed their bees while they tended to their hives.

Notes

- Fruit body is up to 31.5 in (80 cm) across

- Olive-brown spore print

- Appears in summer and fall

The puffball splits open to shed spores.

Trillions of spores are made inside the giant fruit body.

White spindles

Clavaria fragilis

The delicate fruit bodies of this fungus push up through green grass in lawns and meadows that have not had chemical fertilizer added. They can sometimes also be found in the leaf litter at the edges of woodland and in clearings. The fungus feeds on dead plant material. Appearing in small groups, it has several common names—including white spindles and fairy fingers—but its scientific name means "fragile club."

The fruit bodies are often found in small groups.

The club-shaped fruit bodies often have rounded tips.

The clubs are up to 4.7 in (12 cm) tall.

Shaggy inkcap
Coprinus comatus

Older caps are bell-shaped.

The caps can be 4 in (10 cm) tall or more.

This mushroom is also known as the "lawyer's wig" because its cap looks like the curly white wigs worn by some lawyers in a law court. But the cap doesn't stay white forever— eventually, it begins to dissolve into dark ink, which contains the mushroom's spores. This begins at the rim and spreads upward, until all that remains of the cap is an inky puddle on the ground.

Dark liquid drips from the edge of the cap.

The cap rolls upward as it liquifies.

Black earth tongue

Geoglossum umbratile

This ascomycete looks like a black tongue on a stalk, which is how it got the common name "black earth tongue." It is often found in unfertilized grasslands and lawns, but it can be tricky to spot among grass, which can be the same height or taller. Spores are shed from the smooth surface of each tongue. Under a microscope, the spores are long and slightly banana-shaped.

Notes

· Tongues up to 3.9 in (10 cm) tall

· Dark-brown spore print

· Found midsummer through to early winter

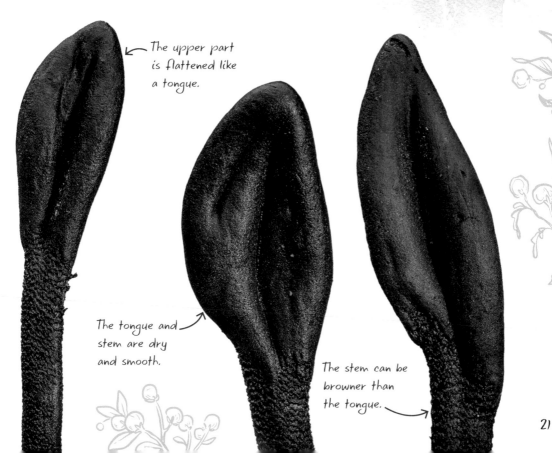

The upper part is flattened like a tongue.

The tongue and stem are dry and smooth.

The stem can be browner than the tongue.

There is often a slight bump (umbo) in the center of the cap.

The gills are thick, waxy, and widely spaced. They are greener closer to the stem, but fade to yellow as the mushroom matures.

Caps are bell shaped and become flatter with age.

Notes

· Stem can be up to 2.4 in (6 cm) tall

· White spore print

· Mushrooms appear in summer until early winter

Parrot waxcap
Gliophorus psittacinus

These colorful waxcaps are grass-green when young, but soon have hints of yellow, purple, orange, pink, and even blue! They are often found in small groups on unfertilized grassland, mossy lawns, and roadside shoulders, and in cemeteries and woodland clearings. The scientific name *Gliophorus* means "carrying glue," and refers to the slimy, glue-like coating on the caps, stems, and gills.

There is a slight red-orange tinge at the center of the cap.

Beneath the cap, the gills are yellow and become paler with age.

Golden waxcap

Hygrocybe chlorophana

This lemon-yellow mushroom has a shiny cap that looks as though it is made of wax—which is why it is called the golden waxcap in the UK. The scientific name *Hygrocybe* means "wet or watery head." This mushroom likes grassland where animals graze, but it can also appear in cemeteries and other grassy areas where no fertilizers are used. In North America it is seen in woodlands.

Blackening waxcap
Hygrocybe conica

The mushrooms turn black over time.

These little waxcap mushrooms are very commonly found in groups in grassland, churchyards, and on shady roadside shoulders. When young, they can be red, orange, or yellow—but they all turn black as they age or if they are touched. They glisten in the sunlight, shiny against wet, dewy grass. They break down dead grass roots, but also partner with mosses.

The cap can be up to 2.7 in (7 cm) across.

The well-spaced gills are pale yellow when young.

Field blewit

Lepista personata

The fruit bodies of this fungus are often found in fairy rings, or in groups packed so close to one another that their caps touch. Field blewits prefer to grow in fields, hedges, and grasslands with chalky soil. The Latin scientific name *Lepista* means "goblet", and the mature mushroom certainly looks like a chunky goblet!

Notes

· Caps up to 6 in across; stems up to 2.4 in tall and up to 1 in thick

· Pale-pink or cream spore print

· Appears in fall

The gills are crowded and do not touch the stem. They are white to begin with but turn pink with age.

Lilac-colored fibers can be seen on the stem.

The mature mushroom has dark-brown scales on the white cap.

The flesh inside the cap is white.

Notes

· Caps up to 9.8 in (25 cm) across

· White or pale-cream spore print

· Appears midsummer and fall

Parasol mushroom

Marcolepiota procera

These spectacularly tall mushrooms look like parasol umbrellas that were used in Victorian times, which gives them their common English name. They are large, fleshy mushrooms and can be found in grass next to woodlands, on grassy clifftops, and on roadside shoulders. Parasol mushrooms sometimes form fairy rings. They are rotters, helping to break down dead vegetation.

The mushrooms are often light brown, but can turn cream if dry.

The cap is shaped like a sombrero, with a bump in the middle.

Fairy-ring mushroom

Marasmius oreades

As well as fairy rings made up of mushrooms, this fungus also causes rings of dead grass to appear by killing the roots. The little mushrooms can easily dry out in the summer, but are rehydrated when it rains. Then they can produce spores again!

The gills are white to begin with, but turn cream with age.

How do mushrooms grow?

Mushrooms are the fruit bodies of just one group of fungi, called basidiomycetes. These fruit bodies appear now and then, but for the rest of their lives the main body of the fungus, called the mycelium, is hidden inside whatever it is growing in. The mycelium is a network of tubes called hyphae. Each hypha is tiny and can only be seen with a microscope. But sometimes, hyphae grow together and form thicker cords that can be easily seen.

Stages of growth

When tiny mushrooms start to form, the delicate gills are protected by a thin skin, called a veil. In *Amanita* mushrooms, an extra veil protects the whole fruit body as it pushes up through the soil.

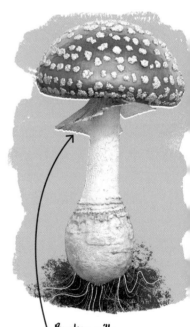

Broken gill-protecting veil
This veil breaks when the cap expands.

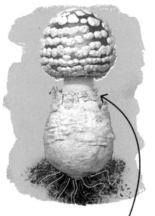

Broken overall veil
This veil breaks when the stem expands.

Young mushrooms
These are completely covered by a protective veil.

Scales
These wart-like spots are the remains of the overall veil.

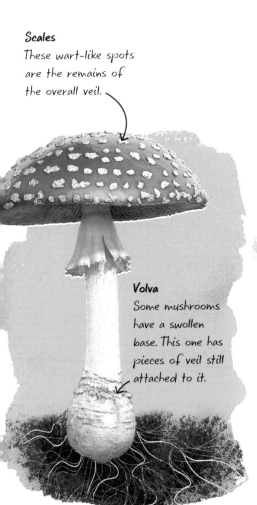

Gills
Spores are made on the gills.

Ring
This is the remains of the veil that protected the gills.

Stem
This raises the cap above the ground to help the spores spread.

Volva
Some mushrooms have a swollen base. This one has pieces of veil still attached to it.

Fungal spores

Fungi spread by microscopic spores, which are so small you could fit roughly 2,500 onto this period. Due to their size, you can't usually see spores to know their color—but many spores falling together onto a surface reveals their color. This is the mushroom's spore print.

Spores can be white, black, yellow, pink, brown, rust, ginger, or purple. They are not always the same color as the gills.

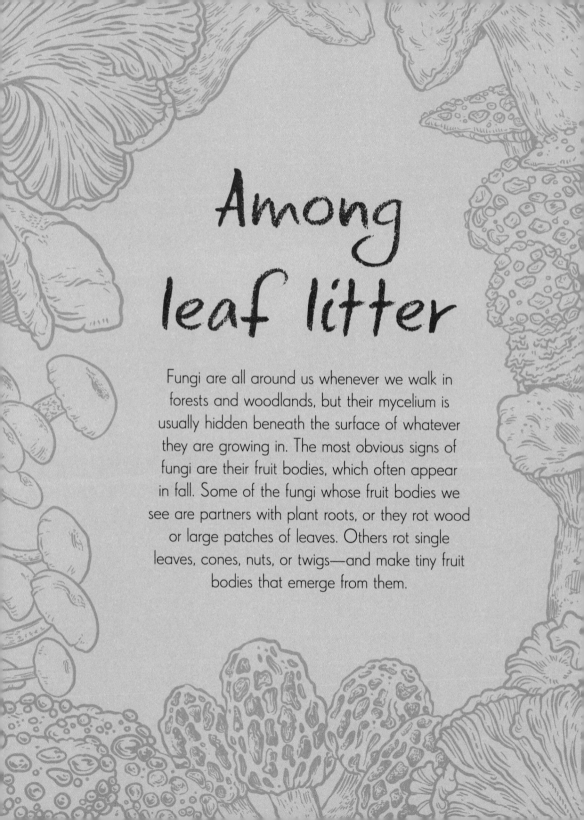

Among leaf litter

Fungi are all around us whenever we walk in forests and woodlands, but their mycelium is usually hidden beneath the surface of whatever they are growing in. The most obvious signs of fungi are their fruit bodies, which often appear in fall. Some of the fungi whose fruit bodies we see are partners with plant roots, or they rot wood or large patches of leaves. Others rot single leaves, cones, nuts, or twigs—and make tiny fruit bodies that emerge from them.

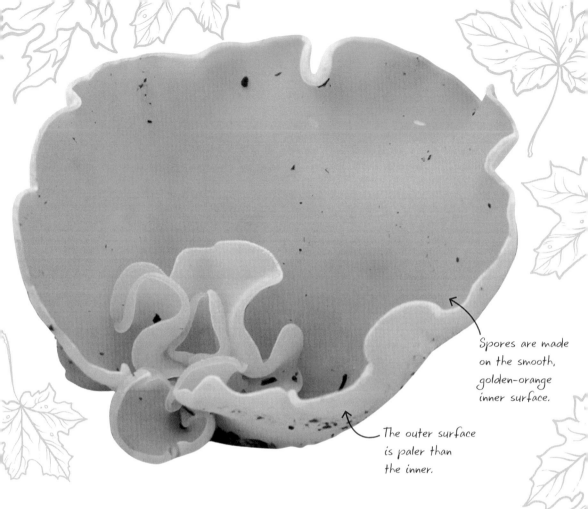

Spores are made on the smooth, golden-orange inner surface.

The outer surface is paler than the inner.

Orange peel fungus

Aleuria aurantia

These colorful cups often grow up through stony soil on or beside trampled footpaths in parks and in woodland. The fruit bodies look like the skin left after peeling an orange, which is how the fungus got its common English name, "orange peel fungus." The second part of the scientific name, *aurantia*, is Latin for "golden." Like other rotters, this fungus breaks down dead plant material.

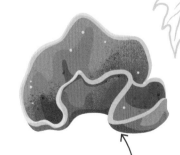

The fruit bodies often split as they grow, so they look like orange peel.

The white warts are the remains of the universal veil, which protected the mushroom when young.

The gills begin white, but turn a cream color with age.

Fly agaric

Amanita muscaria

With its bright-red cap and white, speckled warts, this pretty mushroom is found close to birch and pine trees, often in a ring. It partners with the roots and helps the trees to grow. In the 19th century, people used the mushroom to get rid of flies in their homes. They soaked the cap in milk to attract flies, who then drank the poisonous mixture. The word *muscaria* comes from the Latin *musca*, which means "fly."

Notes

· Cap is up to 7.9 in (20 cm) across

· White spore print

· Appears late summer to early winter

32

Death cap

Amanita phalloides

This mushroom is deadly poisonous to humans, but squirrels and deer eat it. The Roman emperor Claudius is said to have been killed by one when his wife Agrippina added it to his meal so that her son Nero could be emperor. Its fine filaments partner with the roots of oak and other broad-leaved trees. The fungus shares water and nutrients with the tree and receives sugar in return.

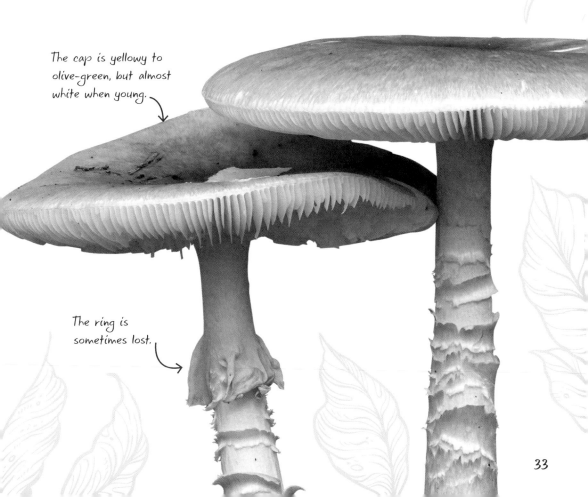

The cap is yellowy to olive-green, but almost white when young.

The ring is sometimes lost.

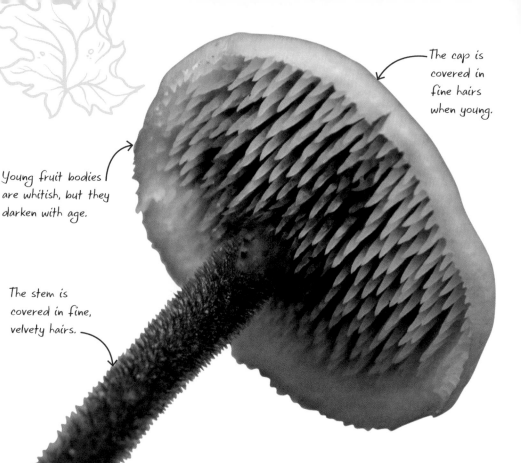

The cap is covered in fine hairs when young.

Young fruit bodies are whitish, but they darken with age.

The stem is covered in fine, velvety hairs.

Earpick fungus

Auriscalpium vulgare

This tiny mushroom is found growing out of pine cones that it rots on the woodland floor. Its unusual, kidney-shaped cap is attached to the stem at one side, rather than in the middle. Underneath the cap are little spines, or teeth, where the spores are made and released. Its Latin name, *Auriscalpium*, comes from the Latin words for "ear" (*auris*) and "to scratch" (*scalpere*), perhaps because it is similar in shape to an old-fashioned ear pick!

Penny bun

Boletus edulis

The cap of this mushroom looks like a type of bread roll called a "penny bun." It grows in broad-leaved and coniferous woodlands, where it works as a partner with trees to provide water and nutrients in exchange for plant sugars. Spores are made beneath the cap in tubes, and the ends of these tubes can be seen as tiny pores. The stem has a white veiny pattern and is fatter at the base.

Notes

· Caps are between 2–12 in (5–30 cm) across

· Olive-brown spore print

· Can be spotted in summer and fall

There are pores rather than gills beneath the cap.

A pale rim runs around the edge of the cap.

Chanterelle

Cantharellus cibarius

The yellow, funnel-shaped chanterelle is different from most other funnels. This is because it has ridges of thick, wrinkled veins under the cap, rather than gills. The fungus partners with the roots of conifers and broad-leaved trees. It can be confused with the poisonous jack-o'-lantern mushroom (*Omphalotus olearius*) and the false chanterelle (*Hygrophoropsis aurantiaca*).

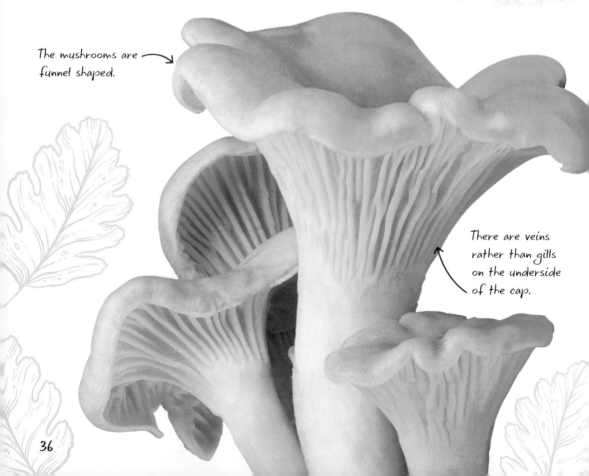

The mushrooms are funnel shaped.

There are veins rather than gills on the underside of the cap.

Clouded funnel

Clitocybe nebularis

This mushroom is sometimes found in fairy rings on the forest floor, in hedges, or even in shrubs, where it rots dead leaves. The rings get bigger each year. Both its common and its scientific name refer to the shape and color of the mushroom—*Clitocybe* means "sloping head" and *nebularis* means "cloudy." A fungus called piggyback rosegill (*Volvariella surrecta*) sometimes grows on top of the fruit bodies.

The cap is cone shaped to begin with, then flattens out-often into a funnel.

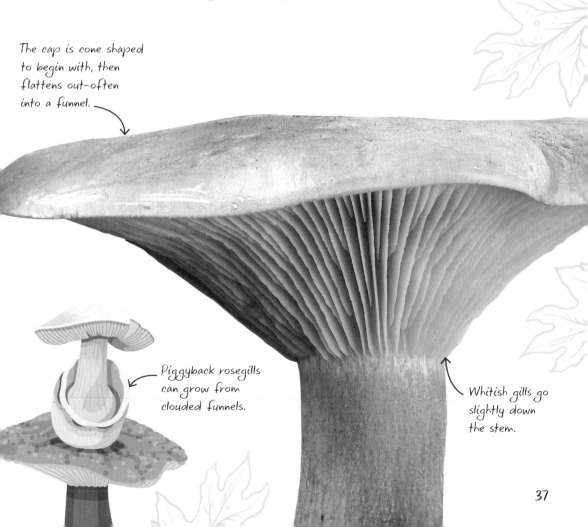

Piggyback rosegills can grow from clouded funnels.

Whitish gills go slightly down the stem.

Aniseed funnel

Clitocybe odora

This mushroom smells strongly of aniseed (licorice), and you can often smell it before you see it. The aniseed funnel grows hidden among dead leaves, on which it feeds. It is found on the forest floor beneath broad-leaved trees, such as beech, and under conifers. Young aniseed funnels are a beautiful blue, which is a most unusual color for fungi.

The cap is often funnel shaped.

Pale gills run partway down the stem.

The young mushroom's blue tinge fades to pale cream as it ages.

Horn of plenty

Craterellus cornucopioides

This black, horn-shaped mushroom grows among the leaf litter of broad-leaved woodlands. The horn of plenty has a tough skin that protects it from maggots, which often eat mushrooms. It gets its scientific name from the cornucopia— a magical horn carried by the mythical Greek god Zeus, which had the power to provide food to all who needed it.

The inner surface is dark brown-black and rolls out at the edges.

Spores are made on the outer surface, which is wrinkled and gray.

Notes

- 1.5–3 in (4–8 cm) across
- White spore print
- Fruit bodies seen from summer to late fall

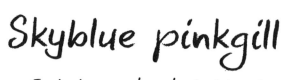

Skyblue pinkgill
Entoloma hochstetteri

Blue is quite a rare color in the fungal kingdom, but this amazing mushroom is strikingly blue. It is commonly found in forests across New Zealand, and is thought to partner with roots of uapaca trees. It is a nationally famous fungus, appearing on the back of the New Zealand fifty-dollar bill and on postage stamps.

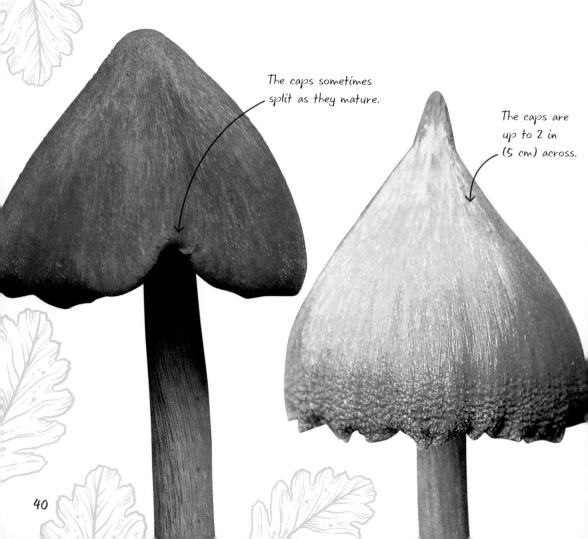

The caps sometimes split as they mature.

The caps are up to 2 in (5 cm) across.

Collared earthstar
Geastrum triplex

This fruit body starts off looking a little like an onion, but as it grows its segments open out into a star shape and its spore-filled sac is pushed upward. There is a collar around the base of the sac, which is why its common English name is "collared earthstar." These gems are often found in lawn borders, where woodchips have been mixed with mulch, or in broad-leaved woods.

The outer layer splits into 5–7 segments, called rays.

Notes

· The spore sac is up to 2 in (5 cm) across

· Dark-brown spores

· Fruit bodies appear after rain in late summer and fall, but can be seen all year

Spores are released from the hole at the top of the sac.

The flesh starts off creamy but changes to brown and cracks with age.

White saddle fungus
Helvella crispa

This rather strange fruit body looks a little like a white saddle on a stalk, which is where it gets the common name "white saddle" fungus. Growing in leaf litter, its white fruiting body stands out against the red and gold colors of fall leaves. It is an ascomycete fungus, which means it makes spores in microscopic sacs on the upper surface of the saddle.

Notes

- Cap is 1.2-3.2 in (3-8 cm) across
- White spore print
- Seen in the summer and fall

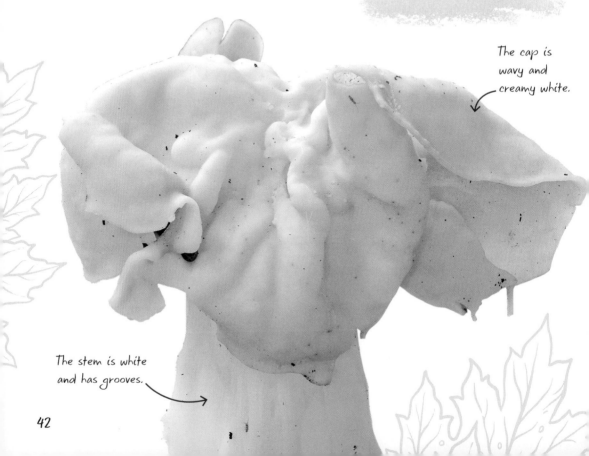

The cap is wavy and creamy white.

The stem is white and has grooves.

Bleeding tooth

Hydnellum peckii

Red, blood-like liquid oozes from the young cap and spines of this fantastical fungus. It stops oozing as it ages, and often changes from a lump-like shape to a funnel. The bleeding tooth fungus partners with the roots of conifer trees in northern forests in Europe and North America. It is threatened by pollution and the loss of its habitat.

Red liquid can ooze from the cap and spines.

The white flesh is sometimes stained pink by the liquid.

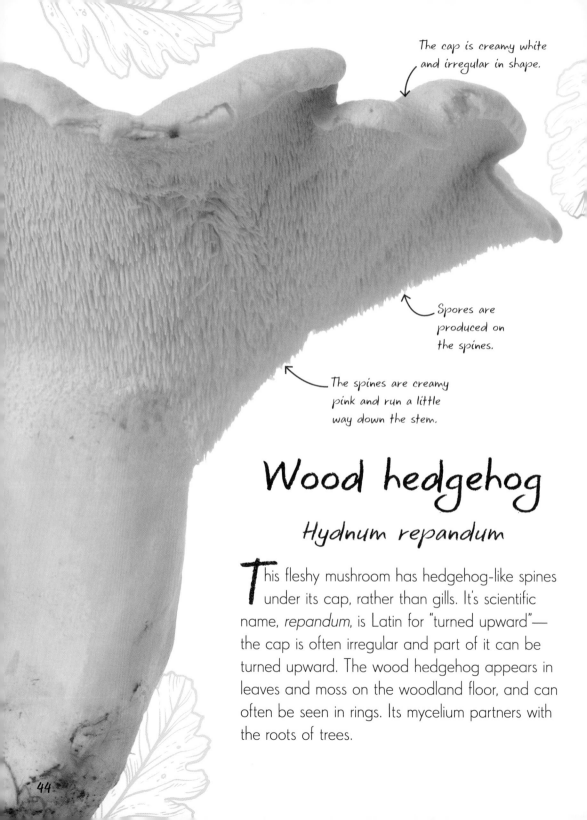

The cap is creamy white and irregular in shape.

Spores are produced on the spines.

The spines are creamy pink and run a little way down the stem.

Wood hedgehog

Hydnum repandum

This fleshy mushroom has hedgehog-like spines under its cap, rather than gills. It's scientific name, *repandum*, is Latin for "turned upward"— the cap is often irregular and part of it can be turned upward. The wood hedgehog appears in leaves and moss on the woodland floor, and can often be seen in rings. Its mycelium partners with the roots of trees.

The gills, cap, and stem are a vibrant violet color.

Amethyst deceiver

Laccaria amethystina

The common name "amethyst deceiver" comes from this mushroom's ability to deceive (trick) us by changing color. It has a deep-violet cap, gills, and stem when wet, but if it begins to dry out, it changes color to pale gray. It can be found in damp, mossy places and among leaf litter on the woodland floor.

The thick, widely spaced gills have shorter gills in between.

The mushroom turns gray when it's dry.

Saffron milk cap

Lactarius deliciosus

These mushrooms have a red or orange cap and bright orange gills. When the gills are cut, they ooze a bright, saffron-orange, milky liquid, which is how they got the common name "saffron milk cap." Part of their Latin name, *Lactarius*, also means "milk producing." They partner with conifer trees and can often be seen in groups in pine forests.

Caps dip in the middle when older.

Gills go a little way down the stem.

Notes

· Caps can be up to 7.9 in (20 cm) across

· Pale-pink spore print

· Appears late summer through to fall

Common puffball

Lycoperdon perlatum

Groups of these pear-shaped fungi are often seen in woodlands—but they can sometimes be found in grasslands, too. They rot dead plant material. When common puffballs are fully grown, a drop of rain or the brush of a passing animal causes a cloud of spores to puff out of the top.

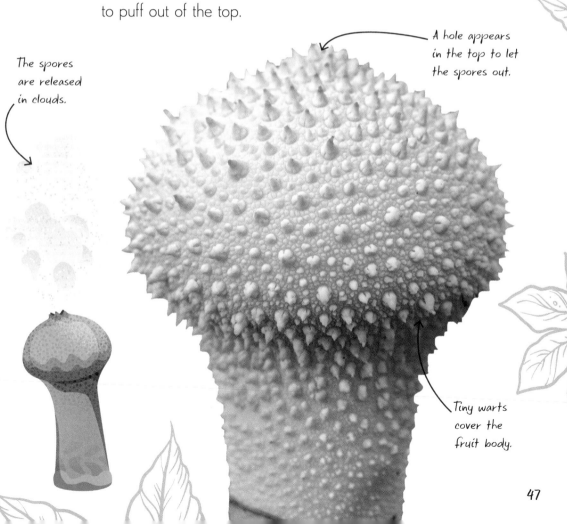

A hole appears in the top to let the spores out.

The spores are released in clouds.

Tiny warts cover the fruit body.

Bog beacon
Mitrula paludosa

In dark, wet places filled with decaying algae, mosses, and plants, the brightly colored bog beacon is always an exciting find. The fruit bodies of this ascomycete fungus poke out of water on boggy ground, looking a little bit like matchsticks with yellow heads. The *Mit* part of its scientific name means "miter," or "headdress," and *paludosa* means "bog" or "swamp."

Notes

- Up to 0.04 in (1 mm) tall
- White spore print
- Seen spring and summer

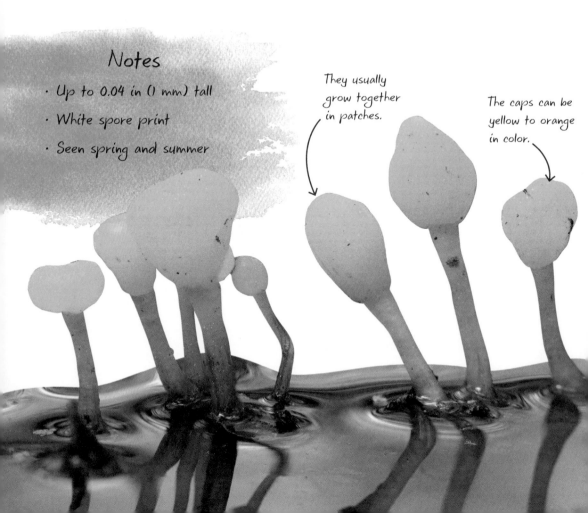

They usually grow together in patches.

The caps can be yellow to orange in color.

Yellow morel

Morchella esculenta

The fruit body of this fungus looks like golden (or pale cream to brown) honeycomb on a stem. Like other morels, it has a hollow stem in which insects love to hide. It often grows on chalky ground, where it partners with the roots of broad-leaved trees, but it can also appear in grassy areas, such as backyards. The yellow morel can be confused with the similar-looking—and very poisonous—false morel (*Gyromitra esculenta*). The two species appear in similar habitats at the same time of year.

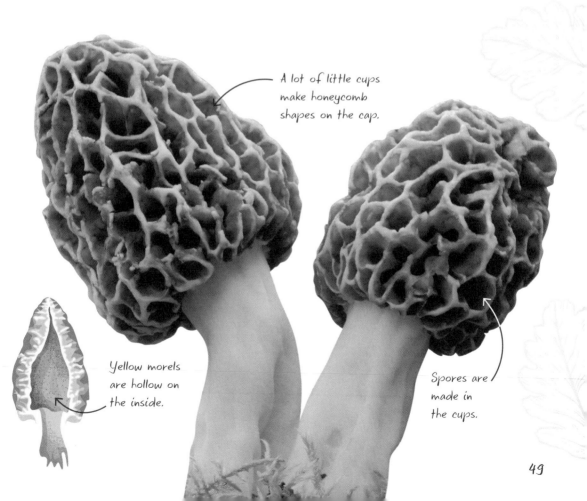

A lot of little cups make honeycomb shapes on the cap.

Yellow morels are hollow on the inside.

Spores are made in the cups.

Veiled lady

Phallus indusiatus

Stinkhorns, such as this tropical species, have an unusual way of spreading spores. They make a dark slime containing spores, which sits on the cap and smells like rotting meat. Hungry flies are attracted to the smell and come to feed. Spores stick to the flies' bodies and are carried to new places when they fly away.

- Cap can be up to 1.6 in (4 cm) across
- Olive-brown spores
- Seen throughout the year

The cap looks like honeycomb after the slime is eaten.

A lacy veil covers the fruit body.

50

The cap is white beneath the dark slime.

Stinkhorn fruit bodies develop from white "eggs" attached to cords.

Stinkhorn

Phallus impudicus

The fruit bodies of stinkhorns grow from a structure that looks a little like an egg, buried in the dead leaf layer on the forest floor. Once the fruit bodies emerge on their stalks, they are less easy to miss—their smell can be detected 328 ft (100 meters) away. This species is found in broad-leaved and coniferous forests.

The stalk looks a little like polystyrene.

Charcoal burner

Russula cyanoxantha

When charcoal burns, it makes a lot of different flame colors, from bright violet, yellow, and green, to brown and bluish gray. The caps of this mushroom can be any one of those various colors, which is why it was given the common English name "charcoal burner." This colorful fungus forms partnerships with trees, and can be found in woodlands and forests.

Charcoal burners can be a lot of different colors.

A slight dip appears in the center of the cap as the mushroom ages.

The white gills are rubbery and crowded.

Common earthball

Scleroderma citrinum

The fruit body of this fungus looks like a small ball sitting on the ground, which is how it got its common English name. Spores are made inside the ball, which then splits open to shed them. The inside turns from white to yellow-brown, and then becomes purple-black when the spores are ready to be released. A rare mushroom called the parasitic bolete (*Pseudoboletus parasiticus*) can only live by growing and feeding on the common earthball.

Notes

· Ball can be up to 4 in (10 cm) across

· Dark-brown spores

· Appears from summer to winter

The common earthball has thick skin and warts.

Old man of the woods

Strobilomyces strobilaceus

This mushroom is hard to spot in the moss and fallen leaves that it grows among in broad-leaved woods, but you won't be disappointed if you spot it! It has large, scruffy black scales on its cap and stem. The scales turn dark brown as the mushroom matures, making it look old and bedraggled—which is why it is called the "old man of the woods" in Britain and North America.

The white-gray pores turn red if bruised and eventually turn black.

Dead moll's fingers

Xylaria longipes

These spooky fungi look like long, black fingers emerging from beneath the ground. They feed on dead wood, which is often buried in the soil. Dead moll's fingers tend to grow in groups, but they can sometimes be found alone. The spores are made in tiny, flask-shaped fruit bodies that poke out of each finger and make the surface look bobbly.

Notes

· Fingers are 1-2.5 in (2.5-6.5 cm) tall

· Black spore print

· Seen all year round, though most common in summer and fall

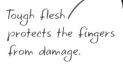

Tough flesh protects the fingers from damage.

The fingers are attached to a narrow stem.

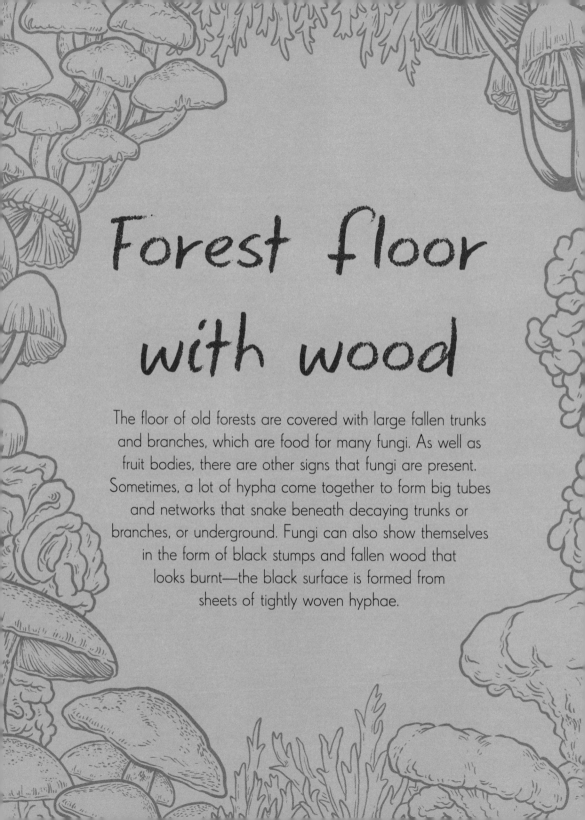

Forest floor

with wood

The floor of old forests are covered with large fallen trunks and branches, which are food for many fungi. As well as fruit bodies, there are other signs that fungi are present. Sometimes, a lot of hypha come together to form big tubes and networks that snake beneath decaying trunks or branches, or underground. Fungi can also show themselves in the form of black stumps and fallen wood that looks burnt—the black surface is formed from sheets of tightly woven hyphae.

Lemon disco
Bisporella citrina

These beautiful clusters of little, vibrant-yellow cups are easy to spot on dead and rotting trunks and stumps in broad-leaved woodlands. They prefer the wood of oak and beech trees. When the cups are wide open, they look like little yellow disks—which is how they got the common name "lemon disco." The scientific name *citrina* is from the Latin for "lemon yellow." The pigment that gives these little gems their color is the same one found in yellow peppers!

Lemon discos are often found in large clusters covering whole branches.

Yellow stagshorn
Calocera viscosa

The little fruit bodies of this fungus look like the antlers on a stag, which is why it was given the common English name "yellow stagshorn." The fruit bodies are a vibrant yellow-orange color and have a waxy texture. In the scientific name, *Calo* means "beautiful" and *cera* means "like wax." This is a wood-rotting fungus, and there is often much more of the fungus buried within the wood on which it is growing.

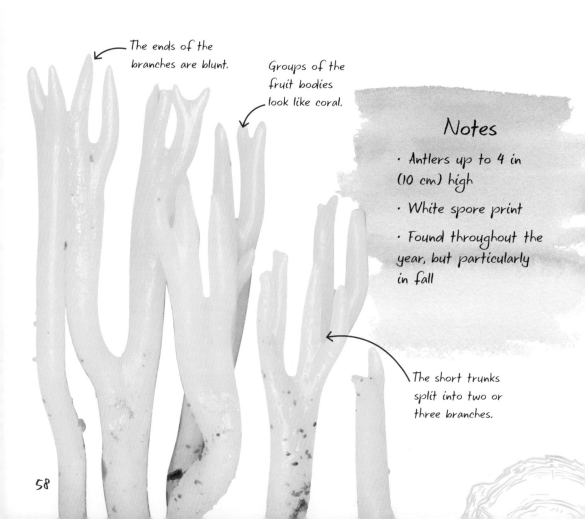

The ends of the branches are blunt.

Groups of the fruit bodies look like coral.

Notes

· Antlers up to 4 in (10 cm) high

· White spore print

· Found throughout the year, but particularly in fall

The short trunks split into two or three branches.

Green elf cup

Chlorociboria aeruginascens

These little blue-green goblets sitting on blue-stained wood on the forest floor are a wonderful find. You can even imagine that fairies or elves might collect dew in them—which is why they were given the common name "green elf cup." The wood is turned blue-green by the fungus, but is hardly damaged at all. Its color is prized by craftspeople, who decorate wooden boxes and other items with it.

The outer surface is paler than inside the cup.

The cups are goblet shaped.

Spores are made on the blue-green inner surface.

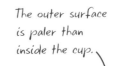

Fluted bird's nest fungus

Cyathus striatus

A white, hairy lid protects the eggs, which eventually falls away.

The fruit bodies of these fungi look like tiny bird's nests complete with little eggs, which could easily be part of a magical hidden world of elves and fairies. When raindrops land inside the cones, the silvery, egg-like spore packages shoot out at speeds reaching 16 ft (5 m) per second. A tiny, coiled cord is attached to each package. When its free end touches a twig or leaf, it sticks to it. The egg containing the fungal spores is then securely fastened to the surface, and hyphae can grow out and feed.

The nest is light brown and fluffy to begin with, and turns darker as the fungus gets older.

There are lines all the way around the smooth inside wall of the nest.

Four or five silvery, flattened eggs sit inside.

A maze-like pattern of slots can be seen on the underside of the fruit body.

Oak mazegill

Daedalea quercina

In Greek mythology, Daedalus grew a maze in Crete to house the Minotaur—a creature that was half man and half bull. The underside of the oak mazegill's cap has large slots with thick walls that look like a maze, so it was given the scientific name *Daedalea*. The other half of the scientific name, *quercina*, means "of oak." It rots the dark wood in the middle of stumps and fallen trunks and branches of oak trees, though it can also grow on wood from sweet chestnut trees.

The caps can be 2 in (5 cm) thick or more.

Notes

- Caps 2.4–8 in (6–20 cm) across
- White spore print
- Seen all year, but shed spores in late summer and fall

Witches' butter

Exidia glandulosa

The story goes that throwing the fruit body of this fungus onto a blazing fire stops witches from casting spells! This folktale, combined with the fruit body's butter-like appearance and spooky dark color, is probably why it was given the common English name "witches' butter." It feeds on dead branches of broad-leaved trees. The fungus shrivels up and turns olive-brown in dry weather, but becomes jelly-like again when wet.

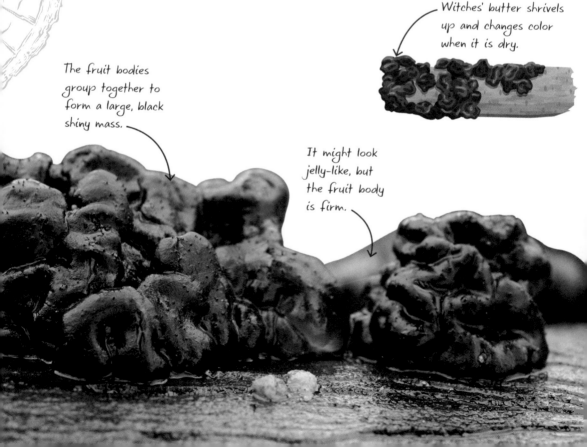

Witches' butter shrivels up and changes color when it is dry.

The fruit bodies group together to form a large, black shiny mass.

It might look jelly-like, but the fruit body is firm.

Ping-pong bat fungus

Favolaschia calocera

Found in damp places on fallen twigs and branches, this fungus was given the common English name "ping-pong bat fungus" because the pretty fruit bodies look like little ping-pong bats (paddles). The underside of the cap has a honeycomb pattern, and *favo* in the scientific name comes from the Latin word for honeycomb, *favus*. The fungus is native to Madagascar but has been accidentally spread to many countries, where it seems to be thriving!

Notes

- Cap up to 1 in (2.5 cm) across
- Stem up to 0.6 in (1.5 cm) long
- White spore print

The pores on the underside of the fruit body are often polygon shaped.

Sulphur tuft
Hypholoma fasciculare

This little sulphur-yellow fruit body is very common in broad-leaved woodlands, though it can be found under conifer trees, too. It grows in tightly bunched groups on tree stumps and other types of dead wood or, sometimes, around the base of living tree trunks. The fungus is an important wood rotter. A single tree stump can provide it with food for several years, before other fungi move in to finish what's left over. It is poisonous to soil insects and humans.

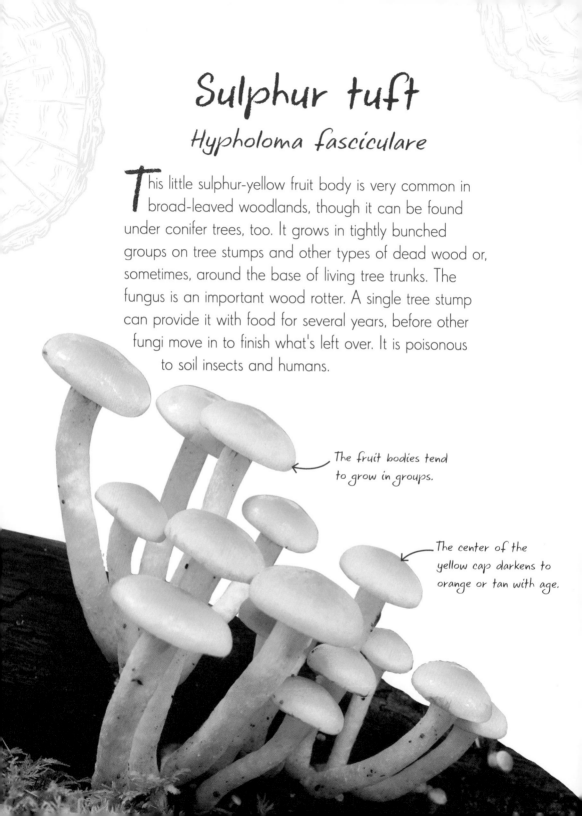

The fruit bodies tend to grow in groups.

The center of the yellow cap darkens to orange or tan with age.

Beech woodwart

Hypoxylon fragiforme

The fruit bodies of this fungus look a like small, brown strawberries, and *fragi* in its scientific name comes from *fragaria*, the Latin word for strawberry. Beech woodwart is very common in Europe and North America. It slowly rots the wood of dead broad-leaved tree branches—especially beech. Its spores can be found in living tree branches, but the mycelium does not grow until the branches die and start to dry.

Spores come out of the top of tiny bumps covering the surface.

Notes

· Fruit bodies are up to 0.3 in (7 mm) tall

· Dark-brown spore print

· Seen all year

The fruit bodies are slightly wider than they are tall.

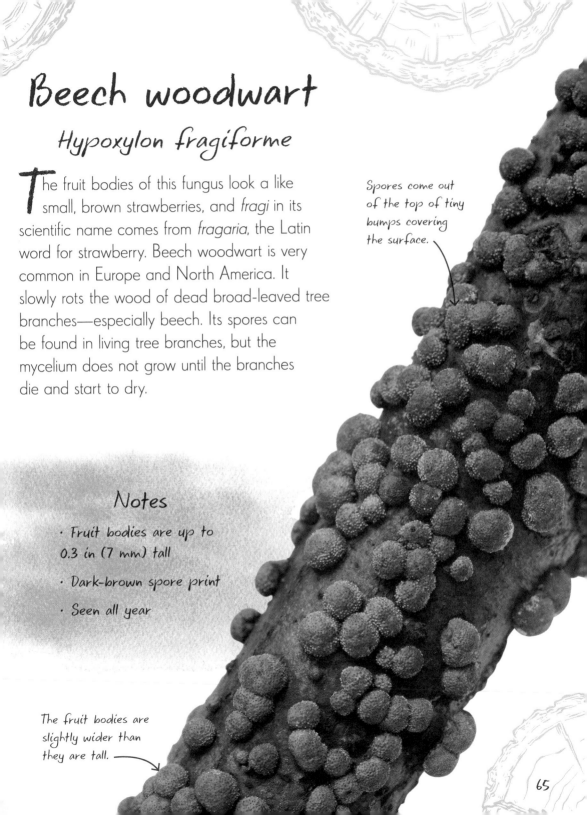

Marasmius tageticolor

The cap of this mushroom looks like a tiny parachute. It is found in Central and South America. Similar-looking Marasmius species are found in cooler places, but this one is much brighter, with ruby red and whitish stripes that look like rock candy. Its colors make it stand out among the leaf litter in which it grows, feeding on fallen twigs.

The cap has red and white stripes.

The gills are spaced quite far apart, with short ones in between.

Notes

· Caps up to 0.7 in (1.7 cm) across

· Stem up to 1.6 in (4 cm) long

· Stem is smooth and beet to ruby red in color

Burgundydrop bonnet

Mycena haematopus

These little mushrooms start out as bell-shaped cones, which open out as they grow. The scientific name *haematopus* is from the ancient Greek words for "bleeding foot"—which describes how the mushrooms drip blood-red liquid if they are damaged. They are wood decay fungi and can be found in small clusters on old decaying oak stumps. Their fungus group, the fairy bonnets, includes the bleeding bonnet (*Mycena sanguinolenta*), which also bleeds—but also includes non-bleeding bonnets.

The pinkish brown color of the cap dries to a pale, pinkish gray.

Red liquid oozes out from cut stems and caps.

The caps are silky smooth.

Dyer's Mazegill
Phaeolus schweinitzii

The fruit body of this fungus looks like shelves growing from the woody roots of conifer trees. Sometimes it grows around blades of grass, which poke out through the shelves. The fungus can kill the conifer and then feed on the dead wood. The fruit body is sometimes used to dye silk and yarn fall colors such as yellow, orange, and brown—which is how it got the common name "dyer's mazegill."

The fruit body is yellow around the rim and reddish brown in the middle.

The tube layer is greenish yellow when young, turning reddish brown as it gets older.

Upright coral
Ramaria stricta

This fungus has a beautiful coral-like fruit body, with pinkish branches pointing upward. In the scientific name, *Ram* comes from *ramus*, the Latin for "branch," and *stricta* means "straight." Upright coral rots the buried wood of both broad-leaved and coniferous trees, but may also partner with trees to swap nutrients, water, and sugars. It is widespread in Europe and North America.

The tips of the branches are pointed.

The coral branches are slim and pale cream to pinkish in color.

Scarlet elf cup

Sarcoscypha austriaca

The bright-red, cup-shaped fruit bodies of this fungus grow on dead twigs and moss-covered logs on the forest floor in damp, wet places, often in the spring. Woodland animals such as slugs and small rodents eat them. Spores are made on the inside walls of the cups, and it is said that a faint puffing sound can be heard when they are released. Folklore tells of woodland elves drinking dew from these dainty little cups.

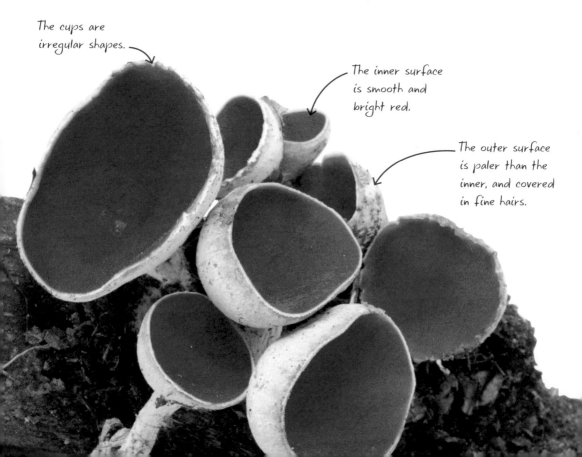

The cups are irregular shapes.

The inner surface is smooth and bright red.

The outer surface is paler than the inner, and covered in fine hairs.

Common eyelash fungus
Scutellinia scutellata

This tiny, bright-orange cup fungus can be found growing on damp, well-rotted plant material, wood, and sometimes horse and cow dung. The fringe of dark hairs around the edge of the cup looks like eyelashes, giving the fungus its common name. The *scutellata* part of its scientific name is the Latin word for "small shield." This fungus can be found in many parts of the world.

Notes

- Usually around 0.15 in (4 mm) across
- White spore print
- Seen in summer and fall

Spores are made on the inner surface of the cups.

Eyelash-like hairs line the edges of the cup.

The top of the bracket is very hairy.

Hairy curtain crust
Stereum hirsutum

This is a very common rotter of broad-leaved tree wood, both on the forest floor and on attached branches. There are often a lot of pale lines in the wood where the fungus lives. The fruit bodies of hairy curtain crusts can have different patterns and colors, but they are usually yellow, orange, or brown. The top side of young fruit bodies are very hairy—which led to it being given the scientific name *hirsutum*, which means "hairy."

Notes

- Brackets up to 3 in (8 cm) across
- White spore print
- Seen all year

The edges are wavy.

Turkey tail
Trametes versicolor

The overlapping shelves of this fungus' fruit body look like the tail of a turkey—so it was given the common name "turkey tail." The underside is white or cream, with pores instead of gills. When found growing on dead wood, the tops of the shelves can be very colorful— but turkey tail growing in dark caves is completely white! In the scientific name, *Tram* means "thin" and *versicolor* means "of many colors." The fruit bodies have been used for centuries to make medicines.

Turkey tail growing in caves is white.

The cap has many different arcs of colors.

The flesh is jelly-like.

Yellow brain
Tremella mesenterica

This yellow fungus looks like a piece of brain, which is how it got the English common name "yellow brain." It feels like wobbly jelly, and that is what *Tremella* means in its scientific name. It is seen on wood, but it is not a wood rotter—it is actually feeding on crust fungi called *Peniophora*, so it is a parasite.

Notes

· Caps up to 3 in (8 cm) across

· White spore print

· Found all year, but most common in fall and early winter

The curly layers of the fungus look a little like a brain.

Plums and custard
Tricholomopsis rutilans

These sturdy mushrooms look amazing when they appear through moss and pine needles in conifer forests, where they rot buried roots, fallen trunks, and stumps. The purple and yellow colors of their caps got them the common English name "plums and custard." The scientific name *rutilans* also refers to their color—it means "turning red." Although the gills are bright yellow, the spore print of this mushroom is white.

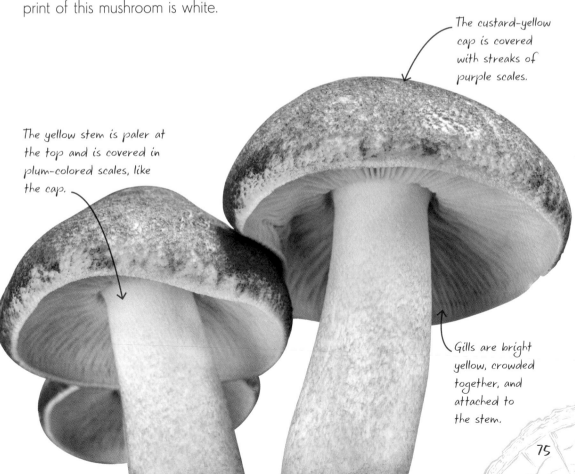

The custard-yellow cap is covered with streaks of purple scales.

The yellow stem is paler at the top and is covered in plum-colored scales, like the cap.

Gills are bright yellow, crowded together, and attached to the stem.

Candlesnuff fungus

Xylaria hypoxylon

In fall and early winter, this fungus turns black—making it look like the wick of a candle that has been lit and put out. It rots tree stumps and other dead wood on the forest floor. The fungus covers the wood in which it lives with black plates of fungal tissue, which look like black lines if the wood is cut. These keep the wood dry—just how the fungus likes it. The scientific name *hypo* means "under" and *xylon* means "wood," which tells us that this fungus is a wood rotter.

The fruit body is white in spring and summer.

The fruit bodies can be up to 2 in (5 cm) tall.

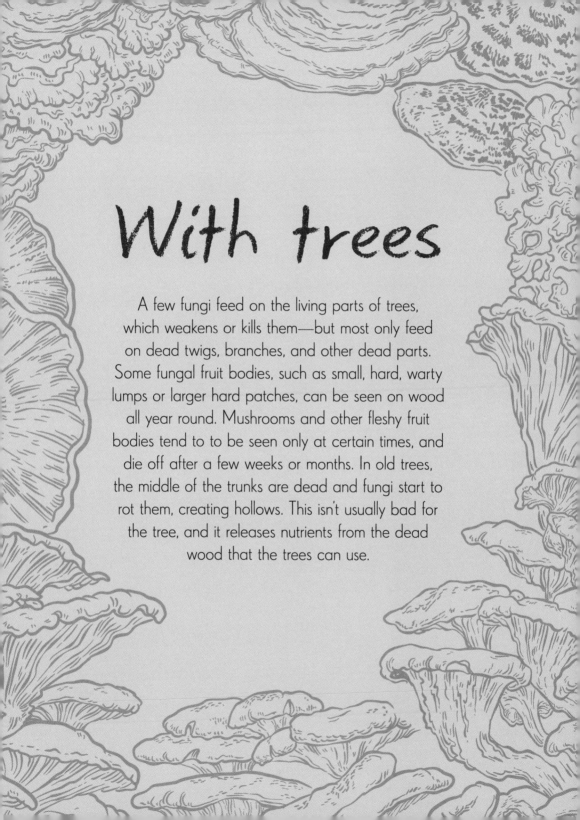

With trees

A few fungi feed on the living parts of trees,
which weakens or kills them—but most only feed
on dead twigs, branches, and other dead parts.
Some fungal fruit bodies, such as small, hard, warty
lumps or larger hard patches, can be seen on wood
all year round. Mushrooms and other fleshy fruit
bodies tend to to be seen only at certain times, and
die off after a few weeks or months. In old trees,
the middle of the trunks are dead and fungi start to
rot them, creating hollows. This isn't usually bad for
the tree, and it releases nutrients from the dead
wood that the trees can use.

Dryad's saddle

Cerioporus squamosus

These very large and spectacular scaly bracket fruit bodies look like saddles when they grow from the side of a tree trunk. They can also look like funnels or horns, if growing from woody tree roots. They feed on the dead wood on which they live. There is a story that tree nymphs called dryads used them as seats in the forest, which is how they got the common English name, "dryad's saddle."

The yellowy brown surface of the bracket is covered with dark-brown scales.

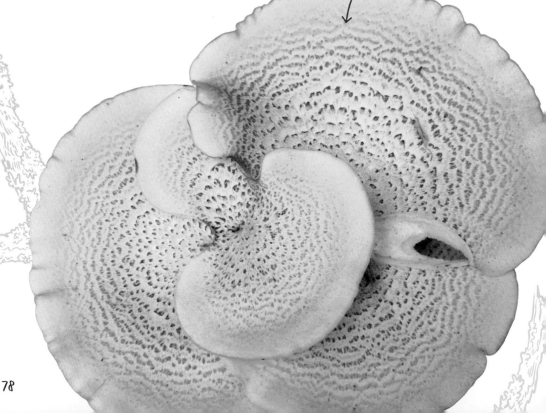

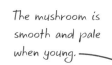

The mushroom is smooth and pale when young.

Darwin's golfball fungus

Cyttaria darwinii

The 19th century naturalist and biologist Charles Darwin collected some of these fruit bodies on his voyage of exploration on the *Beagle*—and the species was named in his honor. The fungus is a pathogen on southern beech (*Nothofagus*) trees, and it is only found at the southern tip of South America in Chile and Argentina. Similar species grow in Australia and New Zealand—a reminder that Earth's land was once connected as a supercontinent!

It grows in clusters.

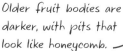

Older fruit bodies are darker, with pits that look like honeycomb.

It grows on branches and trunks of ash and beech trees.

King Alfred's cakes

Daldinia concentrica

What look like lumps of coal stuck to the branches and trunks of trees might be the fruit bodies of this fungus. Its common English name, "King Alfred's cakes," comes from a legend—King Alfred was said to have fallen asleep while baking, and he woke up to burnt cakes that looked like this fungus! Fresh spore-making layers are added to the fruit body for several years, and can be seen if it is broken open.

Inside the fruit body there is a beautiful pattern of concentric layers.

Beefsteak fungus

Fistulina hepatica

When cut open, the fruit body of this fungus looks like raw meat—it even bleeds red liquid. The fungus feeds on dead wood in the middle of the trunks of living and dead oak and sweet chestnut trees, which contain chemicals that stop most other fungi from growing there. It decays the wood very slowly and turns it a warm brown color, which makes it a popular wood for making into furniture.

Notes
- Brackets can be up to 10 in (25 cm) across
- Spore print is pale pink
- Seen summer and fall

Full-grown brackets are a deep-red color.

The underside of the cap has tubes instead of gills.

Hoof fungus

Fomes fomentarius

Shaped like a horse's hoof, this fruit body grows on the trunks of birch, beech, and other broad-leaved trees. It slowly rots the wood. The hoof fungus was found in a pouch carried by Ötzi the iceman, whose 5,000 year old mummified body was discovered in 1991 in the Ötztal Alps, between Austria and Italy. He probably used it as tinder for starting fires.

Notes

· Up to 15.8 in (40 cm) across

· Pale-lemon spore print

· Found all year, but sheds its spores in late spring and summer

A new layer of tubes appears each year, or more often.

The underside is pale and soft, with pores.

The lower
surface
is white.

Birch
polypore

Fomitopsis betulina

This fungus is usually found growing on birch trees. It feeds on the dead wood in the middle of the trunk, turning it brown and crumbly. Alongside hoof fungus, it was found in Ötzi the iceman's tool kit. He probably used strips of the fungus like bandages, to stop bleeding, and as medicine for an upset stomach.

The cap is almost
spherical at first but
flattens out and
darkens as it grows.

Southern bracket

Ganoderma australe

These tough brackets, seen on the lower trunks of trees, grow larger each year. Spores are released through white pores on the underside of the fruit body, and millions are shed in late summer and fall. The fungus rots dead wood in the center of broad-leaved trees, such as beech and oak. Eventually, the trunk hollows out, forming an important habitat for thousands of insects, birds, small mammals, and, of course, fungi.

The brackets can grow to 9.8 in (25 cm) across.

Hen of the woods
Grifola frondosa

The impressive fruit bodies of this fungus branch from a white stalk in wavy layers. It is found at the base of beech, oak, and maple tree trunks, or on large woody roots. It feeds on dead wood, which takes a long time to rot, and its fruit bodies often return in the same place for several years. The fruit bodies look like the layers of feathers on a hen, so the fungus was given the common name "hen of the woods." Its scientific name also describes the shape of the fruit bodies—*Grifola* means "intricate," and *frondosa* means "leaf-like."

Notes

· Can be 3.3 ft (1 m) or more across

· White spore print

· Seen in summer and fall

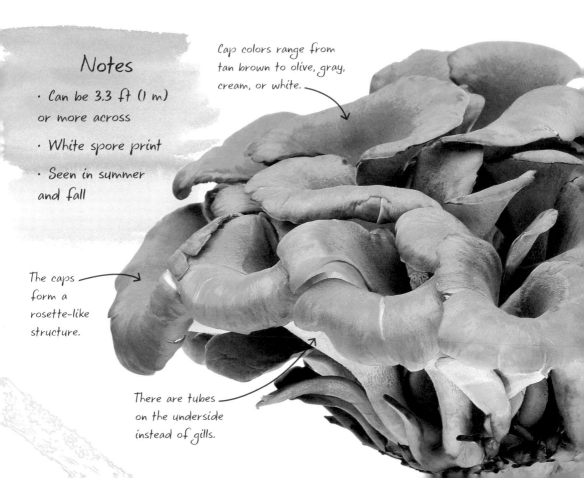

Cap colors range from tan brown to olive, gray, cream, or white.

The caps form a rosette-like structure.

There are tubes on the underside instead of gills.

Lion's mane
Hericium erinaceus

This fungus has several common names, including lion's mane, bearded tooth, tree hedgehog, and pom-pom mushroom. Both parts of its scientific name mean "like a hedgehog." It does not have gills, but makes its spores on spines that hang down. Lion's mane is rare in much of Europe, but more common in North America. It rots dead wood in the trunks of standing and fallen beech and oak trees. In the UK, it is against the law to pick or damage it.

The fruit body is made up of clumps of spines.

Spores form on the spines.

Notes

- Spines up to 2 in (5 cm) long
- White spore print
- Seen in summer and fall

The spines have pointed tips.

Chicken of the woods

Laetiporus sulphureus

The flesh of this fruit body looks like cooked chicken, which is how it got the English common name "chicken of the woods." In its scientific name, *Laetiporus* means "with bright pores" and *sulphureus* means "sulphur yellow color." The fungus decays the dead wood in the middle of the trunks of beech, oak, chestnut, and yew trees—making it crumbly. It forms white, rubbery sheets of fungus inside the wood.

The flesh is bright yellow.

The shelves can grow to be 15.7 in (40 cm) across.

Young shelves are soft and spongy.

Giant polypore

Meripilus giganteus

The huge fruit body of this fungus is made up of layers of fan-shaped caps. It grows at the base of broad-leaved trees, where its mycelium feeds on woody roots. If a tree has been blown over in a storm and had its roots pulled up, roots rotted and weakened by this fungus can sometimes be spotted.

The fruit body does not last long before rotting away.

Porcelain fungus

Mucidula mucida

The fruit bodies of this fungus form in clusters on the branches and trunks of beech trees in Europe—and if they are knocked off, they float down like parachutes. They look like gleaming, upside-down porcelain dishes. The fungus feeds on dead wood, and can also grow on fallen beech branches. Bright orange lines can be seen in the wood, which are barriers made by the mycelium to separate its territory from other fungi. It produces its own fungicide to fight off its rivals.

The cap is very shiny and slimy in wet weather.

The white stem has a ring near the top.

Ghost fungus

Omphalotus nidiformis

This mushroom is bioluminescent, which means it glows in the dark.

This poisonous mushroom can easily be mistaken for an oyster mushroom. It is found in Australia, Tasmania, India, and Indonesia. It decays wood and amazingly glows in the dark. Why certain mushrooms glow is unclear, but it is likely that it is a side-effect of a process that protects the fungus from dangerous compounds that are released when it breaks down wood.

Gills close to the stem may turn green over time.

The gills are pale cream and run down the stem.

Shaggy scalycap
Pholiota squarrosa

This rather scaly, yellowy brown mushroom is easy to spot at the base of old broad-leaved (and occasionally coniferous) trees, and on tree stumps. It is a rotter, and breaks down dead wood. Its scientific name describes the unusual, upturned scales on its cap—*Pholiota squarrosa* means "with upright scales." The mushroom is often confused with the similar-looking honey fungus (*Armillaria mellea*).

Notes

· Caps are up to 4.7 in (12 cm) across

· Rusty brown spore print

· Gills are grayish-yellow but turn cinnamon brown as the mushroom ages

Rings of brown, upturned, triangular scales cover the cap.

The cap flesh is yellowy white.

Oyster mushroom
Pleurotus ostreatus

There are many different types of oyster mushrooms, which vary in size, shape, and color. They grow in groups on dead or dying trees and fallen trunks or large branches. The caps can be cream, pale brown, gray, dark brown, or blue-black—and they often overlap, though each stem is attached separately to the wood. These fungi feed on wood but also eat tiny worms. The caps are shaped a little like oyster shells, which is how they got the common name "oyster mushroom."

Notes

· Caps up to 7 in (18 cm) across

· White or lilac-gray spore print

· Appears in summer, fall, and early winter, and even late winter in warm countries

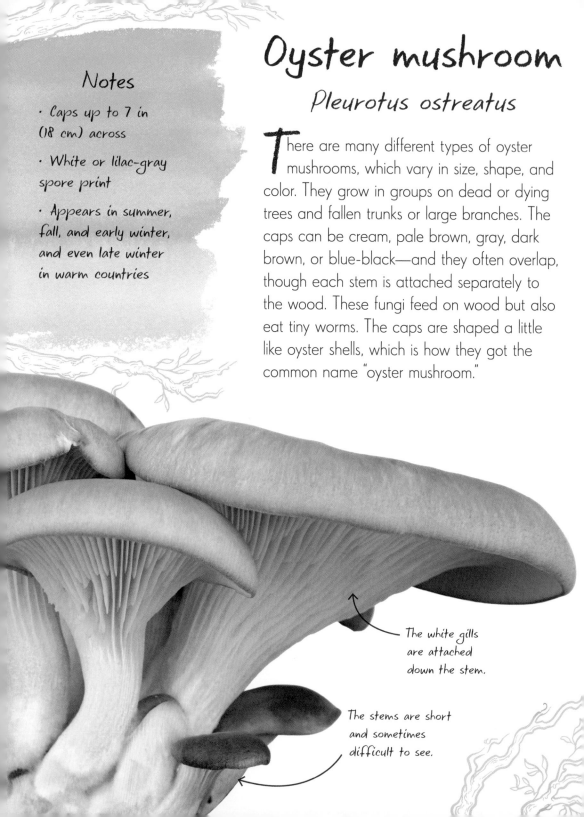

The white gills are attached down the stem.

The stems are short and sometimes difficult to see.

Wood cauliflower fungus

Sparassis crispa

The fruit body of this fungus looks like a very large cauliflower sitting at the base of a conifer tree. The scientific name *Sparassis* comes from the Greek for tear—it looks like it is made of curly, leaf-like folds that have been torn apart. *Crispa* means "waved" or "curly." The fungus feeds on the roots of Scotch pine and sometimes other trees for a long time—often for decades!

The folds turn brown and toughen with age.

The fruit body is shaped like a cauliflower.

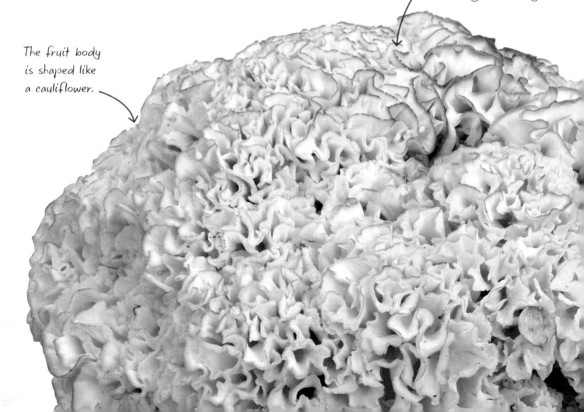

Insect killers

More than a million species of fungi feed on insects, and some are quite gruesome! They can even control the minds of their victims, making them behave in ways that help the fungi spread their spores.

Masses of fungal spores can be seen on the end of the cicada's body.

Massospora cicadina

The spores of this fungus wait in the soil for either 13 or 17 years, until masses of young jumping bugs, called *Magicicada* cicadas, crawl to the surface to start their lives as adults. Spores get onto their bodies, and the fungus grows inside and feeds on the insects. When the cicadas try to find mates, the fungus spreads to them, too.

Chinese caterpillar fungus

Ophiocordyceps sinensis infect the caterpillars of ghost moths as they move through grassland soil, munching on roots. The fungus slowly eats away at the caterpillar and then a fruit body grows from the head. It is a very important fungus in traditional Chinese medicine, and in ancient times it could only be used by the emperor and the people who lived at his palace.

A fungus fruit body emerges from the head of the dead caterpillar and pushes up out of the grass.

Spores are shed from this lollipop-shaped structure that emerges from the ant's head.

The ant host bites into a leaf's midrib (large middle vein), and its jaws lock.

Zombie-ant fungus

Ophiocordyceps unilateralis turns carpenter ants into zombies. The fungus drops spores onto ants as they walk along paths to their feeding sites. It grows into the ants' bodies. The ants get confused, and stagger about 10 in (25 cm) up plants and bite into a leaf. They die stuck to the leaf, and the fungus continues feeding on their insides. A fruit body grows out of the ant's head and sheds spores, which drop onto more ants, and the cycle repeats.

Spores are released
from the tar
colored spots.

Tar spot

Large black spots on sycamore leaves
are caused by the microscopic fungus
sycamore tar spot (*Rhytisma acerinum*).
The fungus feeds on the leaves but
doesn't cause much damage. Spores
are made under the black spots in the
winter, when the dead leaves are
on the ground.

Plant pests

Most plants can avoid infection by fungi.
But if a plant is unable to protect itself,
then fungi will take advantage. They feed on
the living plant, causing powdery blotches,
spots, decay, and sometimes death. Here are
some of the common ones that you might see
when you are out and about.

This leaf is from a
lupin plant infected
with powdery mildew.

Powdery mildew

This group of fungi form a powdery, white
coating on leaves, stems, and sometimes
flowers. They push their hyphae into leaves
to get food from the plant. The dusty coating
on the leaves stops the plant from getting all
the light it needs, so plants infected with
these fungi don't grow as well.

This leaf is from an alder tree infected with a rust fungus.

Rings of spores can be seen on apples infected with brown rot.

Rust fungi

Rust fungi get their name from the powdery, rusty-orange spots they make on plant leaves and stems. There are many types of rust fungi, and they infect a lot of different plant species, from crops such as wheat to garden plants such as snapdragons (*Antirrhinum*).

Brown rot

Look out for signs of brown rot fungus (*Monilinia fructigena*) where fruit trees grow, in the backyard or in orchards. The fungus makes light-brown spore masses in rings around the fruit. These are very common on apples, pears, peaches, plums, and cherries.

Spores are made on black blotches.

Black spot of rose

Black spot of rose (*Diplocarpon rosae*) causes round, black, or purple blotches on the tops of leaves. It is hard to control black spot of rose because the fungus is constantly evolving and rose varieties that were once resistant can become vulnerable to the fungus.

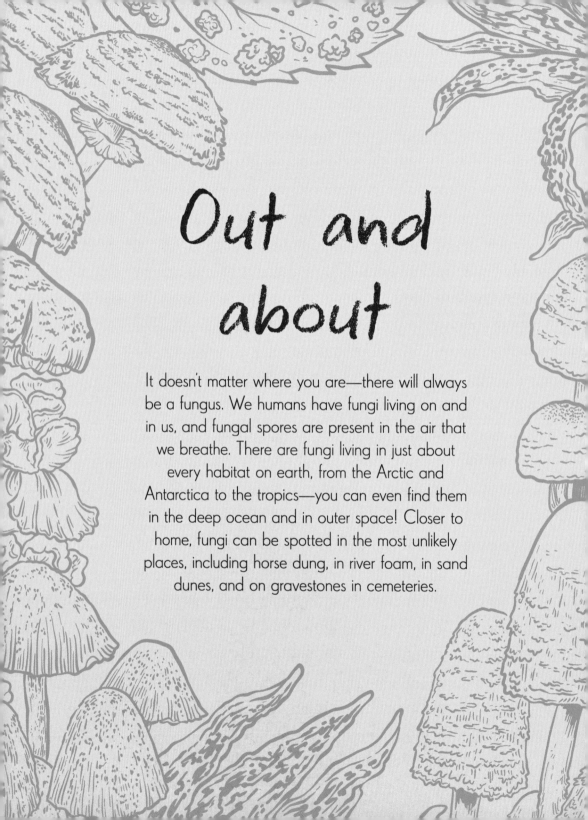

Out and about

It doesn't matter where you are—there will always be a fungus. We humans have fungi living on and in us, and fungal spores are present in the air that we breathe. There are fungi living in just about every habitat on earth, from the Arctic and Antarctica to the tropics—you can even find them in the deep ocean and in outer space! Closer to home, fungi can be spotted in the most unlikely places, including horse dung, in river foam, in sand dunes, and on gravestones in cemeteries.

Honey fungus

Armillaria mellea

The mycelium of a honey fungus can make wood glow.

There are several *Armillaria* species that all look similar. They are honey colored, which gives them the common name "honey fungus." Many of them can kill trees, but some just feed on weak or dead trees. They can spread in soil and under tree bark by making rhizomorphs, which look a little like roots or shoelaces. Their mycelium can make wood glow. In the First World War, soldiers sometimes used this glowing wood to light their way in the trenches.

Scales can cover the caps.

pale-yellow
g can be seen
the stems of
me species.

Spores are produced on the smooth, grayish inner surface of the ear.

The outer surface is brown and slightly downy, with a purplish tint.

Jelly ear

Auricularia auricula-judae

The fruit bodies of these fungi are shaped like floppy, rubbery, jelly-like ears. They grow on the trunks and fallen branches of elder, beech. and other broad-leaved trees. Without rain, they dry up and become hard and brittle. After rain, just like magic, the shriveled ears swell and are jelly-like once more. The fungus can then continue to release its spores.

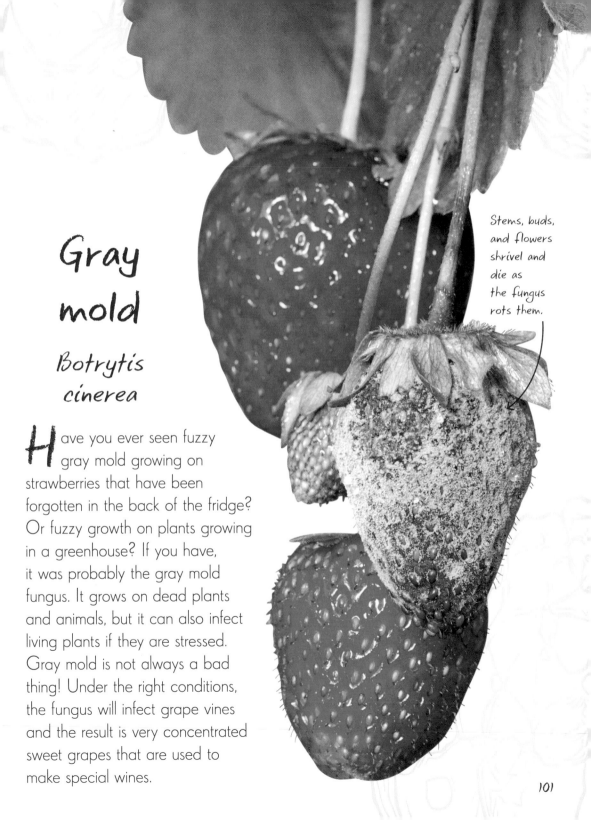

Gray mold

Botrytis cinerea

Have you ever seen fuzzy gray mold growing on strawberries that have been forgotten in the back of the fridge? Or fuzzy growth on plants growing in a greenhouse? If you have, it was probably the gray mold fungus. It grows on dead plants and animals, but it can also infect living plants if they are stressed. Gray mold is not always a bad thing! Under the right conditions, the fungus will infect grape vines and the result is very concentrated sweet grapes that are used to make special wines.

Stems, buds, and flowers shrivel and die as the fungus rots them.

Golden lichen

Caloplaca flavescens

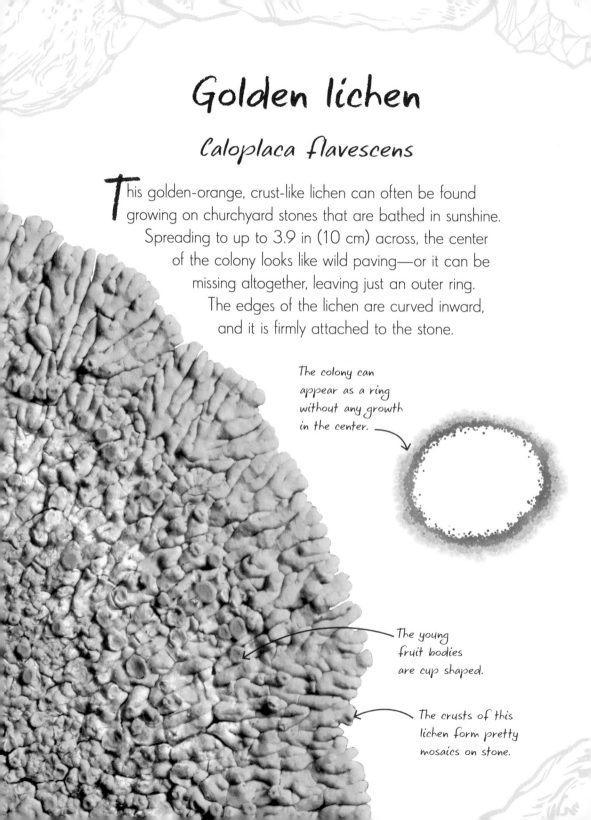

This golden-orange, crust-like lichen can often be found growing on churchyard stones that are bathed in sunshine. Spreading to up to 3.9 in (10 cm) across, the center of the colony looks like wild paving—or it can be missing altogether, leaving just an outer ring. The edges of the lichen are curved inward, and it is firmly attached to the stone.

The colony can appear as a ring without any growth in the center.

The young fruit bodies are cup shaped.

The crusts of this lichen form pretty mosaics on stone.

Shaggy parasol
Chlorophyllum rhacodes

This parasol fungus has a shaggy-looking cap and a thick stem with a fat base. It has a double ring on its stem, which can drop to the bottom. The shaggy parasol is a decomposer fungus and can be found in backyards, parks, and in woodlands. It belongs to a group of fungi called *Chlorophyllum*, which means "with green gills"—though this mushroom has white gills.

The cap has shaggy, upturned brown scales.

The ring can move up and down.

There is a red tinge to the thick, white stem.

Notes

· Cap is up to 7.1 in (18 cm) across

· White or cream spore print

· Seen from summer through to fall

Red pixie cup lichen

Cladonia coccifera

This green and red lichen is often found growing on windy heathland or on sandy soil, and sometimes on wood. It is widespread in North and South America, Europe, and Asia. The main part of the lichen is flat and scaly, with a yellow, orange, or brown underside. It makes upright stalks that are sometimes shaped like goblets. Parts of the top are a red color, and this is where spores are made.

Some stalks are goblet shaped.

Parts of the lichen are bright red.

The stalks are yellow-green and hollow.

Devil's fingers
Clathrus archeri

The fantastic fruit bodies of *Clathrus archeri* look more like an animal than a fungus. It is native to southern Africa, Australia, and New Zealand, but it has arrived in Europe and on the coasts of North America. It rots leaves and pieces of wood, and is starting to invade forests. Like other stinkhorn fungi, it has a foul smell that attracts flies.

The arms are covered in a smelly, dark, slimy mass of spores.

The fruit body usually has four to six arms, though some specimens have eight!

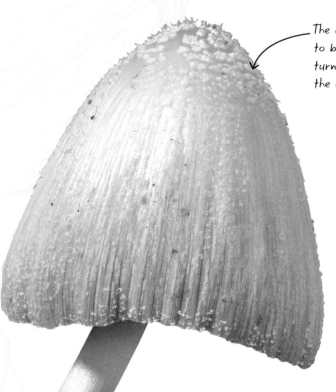

The cap is egg shaped to begin with, but turns bell shaped as the mushroom ages.

The fungus makes a carpet-like mass of orange threads, called an ozonium, on dead wood.

Firerug inkcap

Coprinellus domesticus

If you see fuzzy orange whiskers growing on dead wood, then this could be a sign that the firerug inkcap is soon to pop up—or that the mushroom has already come and gone! It is a decomposer fungus that is sometimes found in damp places in houses. This is how the fungus got the scientific name *domesticus*, which means "home," or "house."

Common inkcap

Coprinopsis atramentaria

This mushroom often grows in groups around the base of a tree stump, or on wood buried beneath grass. The fungus breaks down the dead wood on which it lives. It can lift paving stones and asphalt footpaths as it grows. The spores are shed when the cap dissolves away, leaving an inky liquid. That's how the fungus got the scientific name *atramentaria*, which is Latin for "dark black substance."

Notes

- Cap is up to 3.8 in (7 cm) across
- Spores are black
- Seen from midsummer to fall

The gray cap eventually dissolves into a black liquid.

The cap is bell shaped.

Ridges run from the center of the cap to the edges.

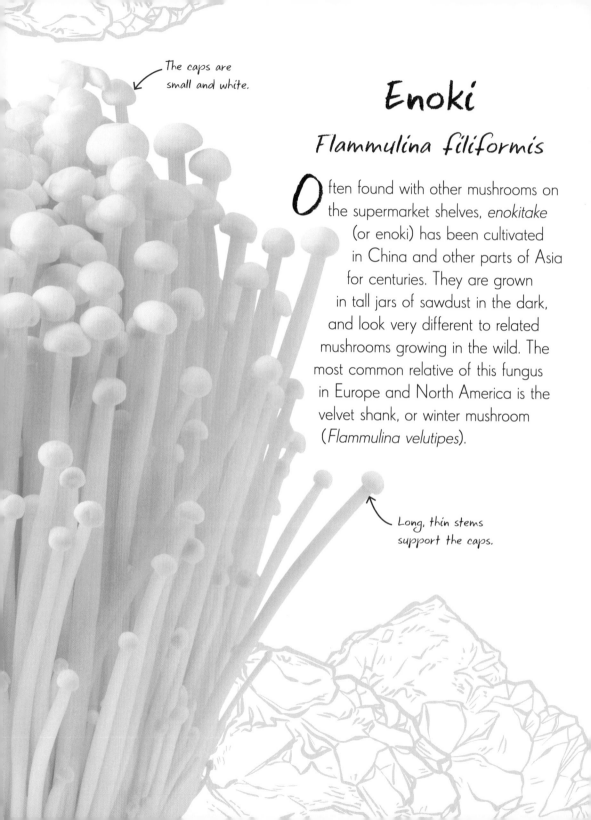

The caps are small and white.

Enoki

Flammulina filiformis

Often found with other mushrooms on the supermarket shelves, *enokitake* (or enoki) has been cultivated in China and other parts of Asia for centuries. They are grown in tall jars of sawdust in the dark, and look very different to related mushrooms growing in the wild. The most common relative of this fungus in Europe and North America is the velvet shank, or winter mushroom (*Flammulina velutipes*).

Long, thin stems support the caps.

The gills turn from white to pale-yellow as the mushrooms age.

Velvet shank

Flammulina velutipes

There are around ten different species of *Flammulina*, which can be found rotting tree branches and stumps worldwide. The scientific name *Flammulina* means "small flame," and was given because of the fiery orange caps of the wild-growing mushrooms. Common names of this fungus include "winter mushroom," because it makes fruit bodies in winter, and "velvet shank," because its stalk is covered in fine, velvety hairs.

Notes

- Caps are 0.8–4 in (2–10 cm) across

- White spore print

- Fruit bodies grow in clusters in the winter

The bright-orange caps are darker in the middle.

Ash dieback fungus

Hymenoscyphus fraxineus

In summertime, on the stalks of dead leaves on the ground, this ascomycete makes its spores. The spores blow up onto the healthy leaves of ash trees. The fungus grows into the leaves, and then into the twigs, and kills them. After a few years, it can kill the whole tree. Millions of trees have been killed in Europe since it first invaded in the early 1990s.

The fungus grows on the stalks of dead leaves, turning them black.

Spores are released from the tiny, goblet-shaped fruit bodies.

Notes

· Cups up to 0.1 in (3 mm) across

· Very common in Europe

· Seen summer to early fall

Shiitake mushroom

Lentinula edodes

This fungus is native to Asia, where it feeds by rotting the dead branches and logs of broad-leaved trees. The Japanese word for "oak tree" is *shii*, and the common name *shiitake* means "mushroom of the oak tree." It is a very popular edible mushroom, which has been grown in Asia for centuries. Shiitake mushrooms are now grown in many other parts of the world, and can often be found in supermarkets.

White scales can be seen on the cap.

The gills are cream or white.

Stinking dapperling

Lepiota cristata

This fruit body can often be smelled before it is seen—and it was given the common English name "stinking dapperling" because of its very strong smell. Like many dapperlings, it is poisonous. It appears in groups in woodlands, and often grows in flowerbeds in damp, shady yards, where it rots dead plant material.

The white cap has a tan-brown center and rings of tan-brown scales.

The stems are smooth and pale, sometimes with fine fibers.

The cap flattens as the mushroom ages.

A delicate ring surrounds the stem, which is easily lost.

The cap starts bright yellow, but fades over time.

Plantpot dapperling

Leucocoprinus birnbaumii

This beautiful little canary-yellow mushroom is common in tropical parts of the world. But it can also be seen in small groups in plantpots, inside the warm greenhouses of colder countries—which is why it was given the common name "plantpot dapperling." It was probably spread as a stowaway with exotic plants that were traded around the world.

Tiny scales cover the cap.

The stem is slightly swollen at the base.

Coral spot

Nectria cinnabarina

Notes

· Coral spots are up to 0.2 in (4 mm) across

· White spore print

· Appears in summer and fall

Each fruit body has a pore for releasing spores.

These pretty, coral-colored spots can be seen on the dead or dying branches of beech, sycamore, and other broad-leaved trees. The fungus kills weak branches and feeds on the dead wood. The common name "coral spot" comes from the colored blobs it makes, which are full of fungal spores. You might also spot reddish-brown, egg-like fruit bodies, which look like raspberries. The scientific name *cinnabarina* comes from a type of rock, called cinnabar, which is a similar color to the fungus.

The fruit bodies are found in dense groups on dead or dying branches.

Common dog lichen

Peltigera membranacea

This is a very common lichen in mild and colder parts of Europe, North America, and Asia. It is found on soil, rocks, tree trunks, and among mosses. It is an ascomycete fungus that teams up with *Nostoc* cyanobacteria. The underside has fang-like structures that attach the lichen to whatever it is growing on. These fangs led to the lichen being given the common name "common dog lichen."

The upper surface has a vein-like pattern.

The blue-gray to brown upper surface turns blackish or green when wet.

Fangs attach the lichen to the surface on which it is growing.

Bright orange-brown, saddle-shaped fruit bodies grow on stalks.

Hat thrower

Pilobolus kleinii

A balloon-shaped structure sits at the end of the stalk.

The spore sac is black.

I t is amazing what can grow in a cow pie! The hat thrower is a fungus that grows out of the smelly surface. It feeds on the poop and makes tiny spore sacs that are shot off at high speeds, away from the cow pie to a new patch of grass. Another cow wanders along, eats the grass, and poops out the spores in a fresh cow pie.

Notes

· Stalks are up to 0.2 in (5 mm) tall

· Spore sacs contain up to 90,000 spores

· Stalks move toward sunlight

The spore sacs are shot off faster than the blink of an eye.

Tropical pink oyster

Pleurotus djamor

This beautiful pink oyster fruit body grows in warm climates such as Mexico, Brazil, and Malaysia. It is sold in local markets, and sometimes in supermarkets in countries where it is not found in nature. In nature, it forms clusters of oyster-shaped fruit bodies on bamboo, palms, rubber, and other trees. It can be grown from kits at home on sawdust, straw, and coffee grounds.

The fruit body can be shaped like an oyster shell or funnel.

The gills run from beneath the cap to the base of the short stem.

Chewing gum lichen
Protoparmeliopsis muralis

This lichen is found worldwide on rocks, concrete, gravestones, and sometimes on the bark of trees. It does well below bird perches because there is a lot of poop, which contains nutrients for it to feed on. The lichen forms pale, green-white, waxy crusts in circles that look a little like chewing gum—which led to it being given the common name "chewing gum lichen." The scientific name *muralis* comes from the Latin word for "wall painting."

The lichen looks a little like a rosette, since it grows out from the center.

The fruit bodies are yellow to pale-brown disks.

The fungus is made up of tiny lobes, which are bigger near the edge.

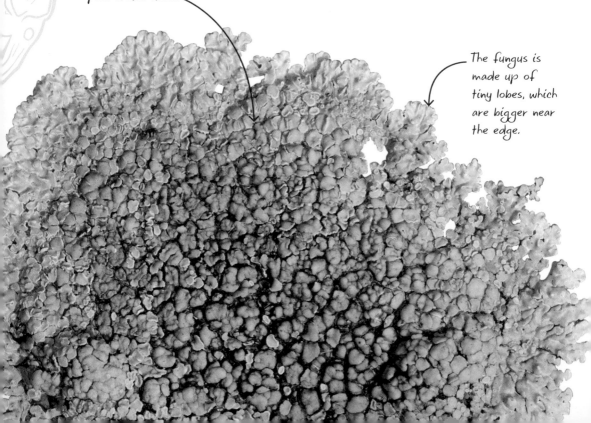

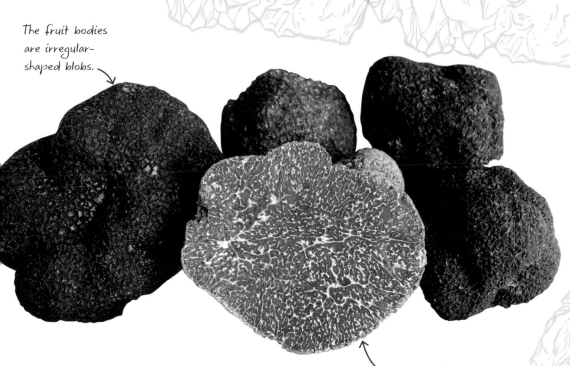

The fruit bodies are irregular-shaped blobs.

A beautiful, white-marbled pattern can be seen inside.

Black truffle

Tuber melanosporum

This fungus is like buried treasure. It grows underground, and is sold for a lot of money as an edible fungus, used to flavor cheeses, pasta, and other dishes. Black truffle (or Périgord truffle) partners with oak tree roots and is commonly found in Southern Europe. The fruit bodies have a strong smell that attracts squirrels and other wildlife. The animals dig them up, eat them, and help to spread the fungal spores in their poop.

Notes

· Can reach up to 3.9 in (10 cm) across

· Cannot grow without a tree partner

· Found below ground from late summer to winter

The fungus forms branches that begin to hang as it ages.

Old man's beard

Usnea wasmuthii

Seeing this magnificent lichen hanging off the branches of trees is a sure sign that the air is not polluted, as it thrives in clean air. It looks a little like straggly hair, which may be where the common English name "old man's beard" comes from. *Usnea* lichens have been used as a medicine for thousands of years, since they can kill some types of illness-causing bacteria.

The cup-shaped fruit bodies look like flowers, as they are flat with petal-like branches around the edge.

Common orange Lichen

Xanthoria parietina

This is a leafy lichen—a type of lichen formed from a partnership between an ascomycete fungus and an alga called *Trebouxia*. It has little orange cups in its center, which are the fruit bodies of the fungus partner. You can find this lichen on rocks close to the seashore, and also on inland walls, roof tiles, or on tree bark. Common orange lichen produces a pigment that can be used to dye wool and cotton.

The cups are darker inside, where the fungal spores are made.

Notes

- Up to 4 in (10 cm) across

- Lobes turn gray in the shade

- Thrives close to bird perches, since nitrogen in droppings helps it grow

The lichen is yellowish green, with orange cups.

Fruiting at different times

Some fungi have always fruited in the spring rather than in the fall. But now some fungi that only fruited in the fall also fruit in the spring. This is likely because their mycelium can now feed in the winter, too.

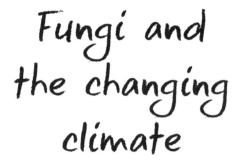

Fungi and the changing climate

*E*arth's climate is changing. It is getting warmer. Some places now have more rain, while others have less, or at different times of year. There are more droughts, more floods, and more storms. This changing climate is affecting fungi. Here are some of the ways different fungi are being affected.

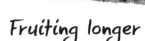

The pestle puffball (Lycoperdon excipuliforme) starts fruiting slightly earlier in the Autumn and finishes fruiting slightly later.

The sulphur tuft (Hypholoma fasciculare) that rots wood now fruits in spring as well as in fall.

Fruiting longer

In some places, the length of time that fruit bodies can be found is more than twice what it was 40 years ago. Fleshy, wood-decay fungi tend to start fruiting earlier in the year. Fungi that are partners with roots of broad-leaved trees now end fruiting later—probably because the trees grow for longer, giving the fungi sugars for longer.

Keeping records

For many years, citizen scientists in Europe have recorded when and where fruit bodies are found. We can look at these records to see whether there have been changes in where fungi grow and when they appear—and we have seen big changes in the last 40 years.

Changing tree hosts

Some fungi have changed the trees they grow on or under. The wood ear fungus (*Auricularia auricula-judae*) was once found mostly on elder trees, but is now found much more on beech and other trees.

The wood ear fungus (*Auricularia auricula-judae*) now lives on different trees.

Glossary

ascomycetes
Types of fungi, such as yeasts and moulds, that produce spores in sacs and have hyphae divided by partitions

bacteria
Tiny living things that can be found everywhere on Earth, such as inside food, soil, or even the human body

basidiomycetes
Types of fungi whose spores develop on tiny club-shaped cells in fruit bodies, which include mushrooms and shelf fungi

bioluminescence
When an organism produces and emits light

bog
Ground that is wet and spongy

bracket
Type of fruit body that is shaped like a shelf or bracket on the trunk or main branches of trees

cap
Structure on top of a mushroom's stem, with gills, pores, or spines on the underside

carbohydrate
Substance, such as sugar or starch, that supplies energy

climate
Weather that is usual for an area over a long period of time

common name
Name of an organism in a local language, used in everyday life, which is usually different to the organism's scientific name

cup fungi
Fungi with fruit bodies that tend to be cup-shaped

decay
State or process of rotting or decomposition through the action of bacteria or fungi

decomposition
Breaking down of dead matter by fungi or bacteria, which releases nutrients

DNA
Substance in the cells of all living things that carries instructions for development, growth, and reproduction

egg
The white ball from which a stinkhorn fungus emerges, or the spore-containing packages of birds nest fungi, which look a bit like birds' eggs

enzymes
Proteins found in living things that cause changes in other substances without being changed themselves

fertilizer
Substance added to soil to help plants grow

filaments
Fine, thread-like fiber found in animal or plants; fungi are made up of filaments called hyphae

fruit body
Spore-making part of a fungus that usually grows above ground—mushrooms are fruit bodies

gills
Thin, flattened, spore-bearing structures on the underside of caps and sometimes also on the stem of fruit bodies

host
Organism that a plant partner or a parasite lives either on or inside and feeds on

hyphae
Very fine threads, or filaments, of a fungus

infect
To cause a living thing—whether a plant, animal or other organism—to have a disease or illness

lobe
A flattish, rounded, protruding or hanging part of a plant, animal, or fungus

molecule
Group of atoms bonded together

mycelium
Main body of a fungus, formed by a mass of fine, thread-like cells called hyphae

nutrients
Food or substance that gives a living thing the chemicals it needs to live and grow

parasite
Living thing that lives on or inside the body of another species, called a host

pathogen
Any organism that causes disease in an animal or plant; some fungi, bacteria, and viruses are examples of pathogens

pigment
Colored chemical or mineral substance

porcelain
Type of thin, white china

pores
Openings of the tubular, spore-producing layer on fruit bodies such as boletes and polypores

root
Plant part that is usually in soil, which attaches the plant to the ground or to a support and absorbs water and nutrients

rot
Decay, or cause to decay, by the action of bacteria and fungi

scientific name
Name of an organism, often in Greek or Latin, from a precise, formal system, which is usually different to the organism's common name

spore
Cell produced by a fungus that can grow and develop into a mycelium

spore print
Print formed from fungal spores, made by allowing the spores to collect on a surface, such as paper, which shows the colour of the spores and the arrangement of the gills. It can be used to help identify a fungus

stem
Main body or stalk of a plant or fungus fruit body, usually rising above the ground

toxin
Poisonous substance

truffle
Underground fruit body of some types of fungi

unfertilized
Land that has not had fertilizer added

virus
Tiny, cell-invading germs that can cause illness and disease; viruses can infect different types of living organisms, including bacteria, plants, animals, and fungi

Index

DK Penguin Random House

Project Editor Kathleen Teece
Project Art Editor Charlotte Jennings
US Editor Mindy Fichter
US Senior Editor Shannon Beatty
Additional Design Holly Price, Lucy Sims, Smiljka Surla
Senior Picture Researcher Sakshi Saluja
Managing Editor Gemma Farr
Managing Art Editor Elle Ward
Senior Production Editor Dragana Puvacic
Production Controller Ben Radley
Art Director Mabel Chan

Editorial Consultant Selina Wood

First American Edition, 2024
Published in the United States by
DK Publishing, a division of Penguin Random House LLC,
1745 Broadway, 20th Floor, New York, NY 10019

DK books are available at special discounts when purchased
in bulk for sales promotions, premiums,
fund-raising, or educational use.
For details, contact: DK Publishing Special Markets,
1745 Broadway, 20th Floor, New York, NY 10019
SpecialSales@dk.com

Printed and bound in China
www.dk.com

MIX
Paper | Supporting responsible forestry
FSC™ C018179

This book was made with Forest
Stewardship Council™ certified
paper – one small step in DK's
commitment to a sustainable future.
Learn more at **www.dk.com/uk/
information/sustainability**

Dr Ali Ashby is a fungal biologist and educator,
based in Cambridge, UK.

Professor Lynne Boddy, Cardiff University,
teaches and researches into the ecology of fungi.

DK would like to thank:
Marie Greenwood and John Hort for editorial input; Sonny Flynn,
Victoria Palastanga, Rachael Parfitt, and Brandie Tully-Scott for design
assistance; Polly Goodman for proofreading; Helen Peters for the index;
Daniel Long for the feature illustrations; Angela Rizza for the pattern
and cover illustrations.